Roe v. Wade

Abortion and the Supreme Court

FAMOUS
TRIALS

Titles in the Famous Trials series include:

Roe v. Wade

Abortion and the Supreme Court

by Deborah S. Romaine

FAMOUS TRIALS

Lucent Books, P.O. Box 289011, San Diego, CA 92198-9011

Library of Congress Cataloging-in-Publication Data

Romaine, Deborah S., 1956–
    Roe v. Wade : abortion and the Supreme Court / by Deborah S. Romaine.
        p. cm. — (Famous trials)
    Includes bibliographical references and index.
    Summary: Discusses the Roe v. Wade ruling which many feel is one of the most controversial decisions the Supreme Court has ever rendered.
    ISBN 1-56006-274-6 (lib. : alk. paper)
    1. Roe, Jane, 1947——Trials, litigation, etc.—Juvenile literature. 2. Wade, Henry—Trials, litigation, etc.—Juvenile literature. 3. Trials (Abortion)—Washington, (D.C.)—Juvenile literature. 4. Abortion—Law and legislation—United States—Juvenile literature. [1. Roe, Jane, 1947– —Trials, litigation, etc. 2. Wade, Henry—Trials, litigation, etc. 3. Trials (Abortion) 4. Abortion—Law and legislation.] I. Title. II. Series.
KF228.R59R66   1998
342.73'084'0269dc21   98-2540
                                                              CIP
                                                              AC

Table of Contents

Foreword

"The law is not an end in and of itself, nor does it provide ends. It is preeminently a means to serve what we think is right."

William J. Brennan Jr.

THE CONCEPT OF JUSTICE AND THE RULE OF LAW are hallmarks of Western civilization, manifested perhaps most visibly in widely famous and dramatic court trials. These trials include such important and memorable personages as the ancient Greek philosopher Socrates, who was accused and convicted of corrupting the minds of his society's youth in 399 B.C.; the French maiden and military leader Joan of Arc, accused and convicted of heresy against the church in 1431; to former football star O.J. Simpson, acquitted of double murder in 1995. These and other well-known and controversial trials constitute the most public, and therefore most familiar, demonstrations of a Western legal tradition that dates back through the ages. Although no one is certain when the first law code appeared or when the first formal court trials were held, Babylonian ruler Hammurabi introduced the first known law code in about 1760 B.C. It remains unclear how this code was administered, and no records of specific trials have survived. What is clear, however, is that humans have always sought to govern behavior and define actions in terms of law.

Almost all societies have made laws and prosecuted people for going against those laws, but the question of which behaviors to sanction and which to censure has always been controversial and remains in flux. Some, such as Roman orator and legislator Cicero, argue that laws are simply applications of universal standards. Cicero believed that humanity would agree on what constituted illegal behavior and that human laws were a mere extension of natural laws. "True law is right reason in agreement with nature," he wrote,

6

world-wide in scope, unchanging, everlasting. . . . We may not oppose or alter that law, we cannot abolish it, we cannot be freed from its obligations by any legislature. . . . This [natural] law does not differ for Rome and for Athens, for the present and for the future. . . . It is and will be valid for all nations and all times.

Cicero's rather optimistic view has been contradicted throughout history, however. For every law made to preserve harmony and set universal standards of behavior, another has been born of fear, prejudice, greed, desire for power, and a host of other motives. History is replete with individuals defying and fighting to change such laws—and even to topple governments that dictate such laws. Abolitionists fought against slavery, civil rights leaders fought for equal rights, millions throughout the world have fought for independence—these constitute a minimum of reasons for which people have sought to overturn laws that they believed to be wrong or unjust. In opposition to Cicero, then, many others, such as eighteenth-century English poet and philosopher William Godwin, believe humans must be constantly vigilant against bad laws. As Godwin said in 1793:

Laws we sometimes call the wisdom of our ancestors. But this is a strange imposition. It was as frequently the dictate of their passion, of timidity, jealousy, a monopolizing spirit, and a lust of power that knew no bounds. Are we not obliged perpetually to renew and remodel this misnamed wisdom of our ancestors? To correct it by a detection of their ignorance, and a censure of their intolerance?

Lucent Books' *Famous Trials* series showcases trials that exemplify both society's praiseworthy condemnation of universally unacceptable behavior, and its misguided persecution of individuals based on fear and ignorance, as well as trials that leave open the question of whether justice has been done. Each volume begins by setting the scene and providing a historical context to show how society's mores influence the trial process and the verdict.

Each book goes on to present a detailed and lively account of the trial, including liberal use of primary source material such as direct testimony, lawyers' summations, and contemporary and modern commentary. In addition, sidebars throughout the text create a broader context by presenting illuminating details about important points of law, information on key personalities, and important distinctions related to civil, federal, and criminal procedures. Thus, all of the primary and secondary source material included in both the text and the sidebars demonstrates to readers the sources and methods historians use to derive information and conclusions about such events.

Lastly, each *Famous Trials* volume includes one or more of the following comprehensive tools that motivate readers to pursue further reading and research. A timeline allows readers to see the scope of the trial at a glance, annotated bibliographies provide both sources for further research and a thorough list of works consulted, a glossary helps students with unfamiliar words and concepts, and a comprehensive index permits quick scanning of the book as a whole.

The insight of Oliver Wendell Holmes Jr., distinguished Supreme Court justice, exemplifies the theme of the *Famous Trials* series. Taken from *The Common Law*, published in 1881, Holmes remarked: "The life of the law has not been logic, it has been experience." That "experience" consists mainly in how laws are applied in society and challenged in the courts, a process resulting in differing outcomes from one generation to the next. Thus, the *Famous Trials* series encourages readers to examine trials within a broader historical and social context.

Introduction

A Watershed Case

THE U.S. SUPREME COURT'S 1973 ruling in *Roe v. Wade* legalized abortion throughout the United States. It found that the U.S. Constitution's Ninth Amendment protected a woman's right to seek an abortion as an "unenumerated" right. The ruling culminated more than half a century of struggle that pitted women and moral standards against one another in matters of birth control and family planning. In establishing a woman's right to abort an unwanted pregnancy, the ruling affirmed that abortion was a method of contraception and as such was a medical matter between a woman and her physician. This made abortion, like other medical decisions, an individual and private concern that belonged beyond the intruding reach of the law.

Unsettling Established Principles

Roe v. Wade also affirmed an important concept that first surfaced in Supreme Court rulings more than half a century earlier: The U.S. Constitution protects both expressed, or enumerated, and unexpressed, or unenumerated, rights. The right to keep and bear arms, for example, is an *enumerated* right. The Constitution specifically identifies this right, and explains why it is a right, in the Second Amendment, which says, "the right of the people to keep and bear Arms shall not be infringed."

The right to privacy, under which falls a woman's right to make decisions regarding the use of her body, is implied, though not expressed; it is an *unenumerated* right. Nowhere in the Constitution does it specifically say that every American citizen has

9

the right to privacy. Yet the Supreme Court has consistently accepted that the Constitution and its amendments both address and extend protection to the right to privacy, as well as other unenumerated rights. Rulings that do so most often cite the Ninth Amendment, which says: "The enumeration in the Constitution, of certain rights, shall not be construed to deny or disparage others retained by the people."

In his book *A History of the Supreme Court,* historian Bernard Schwartz identifies *Roe v. Wade* as one of only four "watershed" rulings made by the Court in its post-Constitution history. Schwartz borrowed the definition from the famous jurist Oliver Wendell Holmes, who served as Supreme Court justice from 1902 to 1932. Such rulings, said Holmes, "work like the pressure of water flowing down a mountain from a watershed, casting doubts on what had previously seemed clear and causing even well-settled principles of law to change."

Roe v. Wade has done more than unsettle established principles. The ruling ignited a nationwide debate that has raged, at times violently, for more than a quarter of a century since it was handed down. It is indisputably the most controversial decision the Court has ever rendered. At its heart are two crucial questions:

• Does a woman have an unequivocal right to decisions regarding her body, even when those decisions affect another life?

• Does the U.S. Constitution define and protect this right?

Whose Rights Count?

Abortion is a deeply emotional and moral matter for many people. Most people who support a woman's right to choose abortion are uncomfortable thinking about abortion as the taking of a human life. Supporters endorse the concept of free choice—a woman's right to make choices about her body—more so than abortion itself. The Constitution protects this right, they say, through the Fourth, Ninth, and Fourteenth Amendments. Those who oppose abortion, and *Roe v. Wade* as the vehicle for legalizing the procedure, do so primarily as a matter of defending the "right to life" of the unborn fetus. Abortion is not a matter of choice or privacy, opponents say, but rather an issue of sacrificing one set of rights for another.

RELEVANT CONSTITUTIONAL AMENDMENTS

The attorneys representing Jane Roe based their arguments on several key constitutional amendments. The First and Fifth Amendments offer broad protections generally referred to as "due process" rights. These rights granted Jane Roe the ability to bring her case to the courts for consideration and judgment.

A pivotal argument for the Roe attorneys centered around unenumerated rights. The Ninth Amendment protected such rights, they said, which included a woman's right to make decisions about reproduction.

While the Fourteenth Amendment also contains a due process reference, the attorneys included it because of a clause restricting states from passing laws that infringe upon constitutional rights. The Fourth Amendment was invoked as a constitutional guarantee of privacy. They argued that previous Court rulings extended this right to safeguard the relationship between a patient and a physician. Abortion, they said, was both a medical decision and a matter of reproductive rights. This amendment prohibits states from passing laws that prevent a woman from exercising her rights in these areas. The *Roe* attorneys believed that laws outlawing abortion imposed restrictions on the constitutionally guaranteed rights of women, therefore making the laws unconstitutional. (The excerpts from the amendments include the aspects most important to *Roe v. Wade* in italics.)

First Amendment—Congress shall make no law respecting an establishment of religion, or prohibiting the free exercise thereof; or abridging the freedom of speech, or of the press; or the right of the people peaceably to assemble, and *to petition the Government for a redress of grievances.*

Fourth Amendment—*The right of the people to be secure in their persons, houses, papers, and effects, against unreasonable searches and seizures, shall not be violated.*

Fifth Amendment—No person shall be . . . *deprived of life, liberty, or property, without due process of law.*

Ninth Amendment—*The enumeration in the Constitution, of certain rights, shall not be construed to deny or disparage others retained by the people.*

Fourteenth Amendment, Section 1—*No State shall make or enforce any law which shall abridge the privileges or immunities of citizens of the United States; nor shall any State deprive any person of life, liberty, or property, without due process of law; nor deny to any person within its jurisdiction the equal protection of the laws.*

Although many religious belief systems establish the beginning of life as the time of conception, neither science nor law has yet done so. Science presents the argument that life in fact exists before conception, since both the ovum and the sperm are living cells. Technology that was once the stuff of science fiction has become reality since *Roe v. Wade.* Today viability (the ability of the fetus to survive outside the womb) is even less clearly defined as fertility researchers close in on the capability to remove a fetus from the womb at an early gestational age and bring it to full term in a laboratory setting. American law accepts the presumption that life begins at birth, however, leaving the rights of the fetus ambiguous.

There have been numerous attempts to regulate or restrict abortion, particularly in the second and third trimesters when viability becomes a tangible issue. Public opinion polls consistently

Abortion protesters in the 1970s disagree with the Supreme Court's Roe v. Wade *presumption that life begins at birth.*

show that the majority of Americans favor abortion with some restrictions. Such restrictions often include limiting access to abortion for minors, limiting abortion to circumstances of rape or in which the fetus has severe birth defects or the pregnancy endangers the mother's life, and prohibiting abortion after a certain fetal age. Other legal challenges have sought to overturn *Roe v. Wade* altogether, arguing that the fetus's right to life outweighs any rights to choice on the mother's part.

Most arguments opposing the *Roe* decision say the states should have the right to enact laws that reflect the desires of their populations, including laws that entirely outlaw abortion if that is what the people want. Those who defend *Roe v. Wade* argue that what the people want is not necessarily right, good for them, or good for the country as a whole. In fact, say *Roe* supporters, the Constitution exists precisely to protect the greater good by establishing certain fundamental principles that cannot be altered except by universal consensus. The only way these principles should be altered, say supporters, is through the constitutional amendment process to assure that all Americans have an opportunity to express their views. So far, attempts to pass such an amendment have been unsuccessful.

It's Not Just About Abortion

Despite the loud and angry clashes that still flare in legislatures and public meeting halls across the nation, the legalization of abortion is only one consequence, and some say a relatively minor one, of *Roe v. Wade*. The ruling achieved what many legal analysts and constitutional experts say is a result far more significant than permitting the act of abortion. *Roe v. Wade* definitively established, for the first time in judicial history, constitutional protection for unenumerated rights—those rights that are not specifically identified in the U.S. Constitution yet to which all Americans are entitled without restriction from state and local intervention.

While a complete reversal of *Roe v. Wade* would not automatically make abortion illegal, it would return to the states the ability to outlaw abortion. It would also effectively establish a narrow, literal interpretation of the Constitution confined to *enumerated* rights. In a world of only enumerated rights, there would be no right to privacy or to the many freedoms Americans have come to enjoy. In such an environment, *Roe* supporters point out, there in fact would be no constitutional protection to prevent states from *mandating* abortions if they so chose—or, for that matter, sterilization and other means of reproductive control.

Such a scenario may seem far-fetched in today's America. In other countries and cultures where overpopulation threatens survival, however, it is a way of life. Laws in China, for example, limit the number of children a married couple may have, and permit forced abortions for those who violate the law. Some provinces of China also require the sterilization of those with severe mental retardation. Critics of such laws condemn them as human rights violations, charging that they lead to other atrocities as well, such as infanticide (killing newborn babies).

America's own history yields its share of well-intended though equally repugnant laws. A Supreme Court decision in 1927, for example, upheld the right of the state of Virginia to involuntarily sterilize "imbeciles," or individuals considered "retarded." Many of the individuals lumped together under this label might not even be considered mentally handicapped by contemporary standards. However, local courts used the Virginia law to force sterilization in such situations until 1972, just a year before *Roe v. Wade.*

The U.S. Constitution does not specifically and explicitly prevent intrusions into what Americans

A 1973 photo shows pro-choice demonstrators supporting a woman's right to terminate her pregnancy.

have come to regard as their right to privacy. Protection instead comes from decisions rendered in landmark cases such as *Griswold v. Connecticut, Mapp v. Ohio,* and *Roe v. Wade*—all cases that forced the Supreme Court to evaluate both the *content* and the *intent* of the Constitution to safeguard personal privacy. The extended protections such rulings establish are the underpinnings of what defines freedom in America today. It is these underpinnings, say constitutional law experts, that are what is really at stake as the abortion battle rages on. *Roe v. Wade* is not just about abortion. *Roe v. Wade* is about the much broader issues of personal rights and privacy.

Chapter 1

A Trip to Mexico
Starts a Journey to the
U.S. Supreme Court

IN 1967, A YOUNG FEMALE law student in Texas confronted the issue of unenumerated rights in a personal way when she found herself facing an unexpected and undesired pregnancy. The situation jeopardized her entire future—she was about to graduate from law school, and her husband-to-be had just started. The couple's plans did not include children, even after marriage. After carefully considering the options available to them, they decided to seek an abortion.

In Texas, as in forty-five other states at the time, abortion was illegal. The couple's decision to obtain one meant a trip across the border to a dusty little Mexican town where abortions, though also illegal, were available for the right price. The couple located a doctor with a reputation for clean facilities and competent care, and on a Friday morning they drove south of Austin to a small town a few miles within Mexico. Fortunately the doctor's reputation was deserved and the two were back in class on Monday morning, their weekend absence unnoticed.

That weekend in Mexico remained a vivid memory for the woman. After she received her law degree and married the man who had shared the experience, she became active in women's groups that provided information about issues such as birth control and abortion. With encouragement from others in those

16

groups and from lawyer friends who shared her belief that laws prohibiting abortion were unconstitutional, the young lawyer determined she would find a case to force the courts to consider the matter. Less than two years later, she did so.

The Search for Jane Roe

The young lawyer was Sarah Weddington. As her interest in challenging Texas antiabortion laws grew, Weddington realized she would need help to find a case that had strong legal standing—that is, one that contained all the elements that would propel it to the desired outcome of having such laws declared unconstitutional. She remembered a former law school classmate, Linda Coffee, who had a reputation as a brilliant legal mind. Weddington contacted her for guidance and assistance. Believing the right case could affect abortion laws nationwide, Coffee agreed to join the effort.

Their research into abortion prohibitions led the two attorneys to conclude that any case challenging these prohibitions would fare best in federal court. There, the lawyers could attack the constitutionality of the Texas abortion laws. They felt the ideal venue would be a federal district court whose judges were accustomed to hearing constitutional challenges. The case would have to do more than just ask for the court's opinion. It would have to feature a plaintiff who could clearly demonstrate "a genuine case or controversy" and a "direct and significant effect" from the law in question. These were two critical legal criteria for challenging laws

Fighting antiabortion laws held personal significance for Sarah Weddington, who sought an abortion in Mexico while still a student in law school.

on the basis of constitutionality. This meant the pair needed a pregnant woman who desired but could not obtain an abortion, and who would agree to take the matter forward in a lawsuit. They put out the word to their network of lawyers and activists, then waited.

The first response came in early December 1969 from a lawyer friend of Coffee's, Henry McClaskey. A woman had come to his office seeking assistance in locating an abortionist, he said. McClaskey explained to the woman that he handled adoptions, not abortions. He had heard of Weddington's quest for a plaintiff, however, and so he gave the woman her name.

Within a week of McClaskey's call, Weddington and Coffee met with their potential plaintiff in Dallas. From the beginning, the lawyers had doubts. The woman who met them was hesitant, almost suspicious. She wanted an abortion and was willing to go to court if doing so would help her obtain one. She wasn't particularly interested in the legal or constitutional aspects of the matter, however, and did not seem to understand the potential magnitude of a lawsuit. She wasn't entirely clear on the circumstances of her pregnancy, offering sometimes conflicting stories.

In her book, *A Question of Choice*, Weddington describes that meeting in a local restaurant and her first impressions of the woman who would become Jane Roe.

> She was petite, with an upturned nose. She was wearing jeans and an oversize blouse that was not tucked in, peasant style. She was outgoing and talked easily. After initial chitchat, I told her about our ultimate goal: to be a part of the national efforts to make abortion a woman's choice and a safe medical procedure. . . . She explained that she was pregnant and did not want to go through with the pregnancy. She had had a rough life: She already had one child and did not want another. Her mother had taken her daughter away from her and she seldom got to see her. She had never finished the tenth grade, was working as a waitress, and knew she would lose her job if the pregnancy continued.

A 1989 photo of the woman known as Jane Roe, the plaintiff in the Roe v. Wade *case.*

Weddington and Coffee had to inform the Dallas woman that her case would probably not move through the courts quickly enough for her to obtain the abortion she wanted. Deeply disappointed, the woman reluctantly agreed to let the two lawyers present her case anyway. To protect her identity, Weddington and Coffee decided to file the case anonymously and call their plaintiff Jane Roe.

Though excited to have found someone willing to act as plaintiff in the case, Weddington and Coffee knew Jane Roe had no real interest in the case beyond her own situation. They also knew she was unsettled in her life. She changed jobs and moved frequently. The attorneys feared that their client's transient lifestyle meant they could lose track of her before the case went to court and they would have to start over.

As they talked through the various scenarios that could result if their plaintiff disappeared before the case went to trial, the lawyers received another contact. A married couple had heard that Coffee was looking for a plaintiff to challenge the Texas abortion law. The woman had serious medical problems that made pregnancy, as well as taking the new hormone-based birth control pill, dangerous for her. She and her husband had already made one trip to Mexico for an illegal abortion.

Coffee and Weddington were excited to talk with the couple. Adding them to the case would give the case a broader base. Jane Roe was a single woman, not only pregnant out of wedlock but also uncertain of who had fathered her child. While the attorneys sheltered their client under the cloak of anonymity, they knew the court could order them to produce Jane Roe for direct questioning. Any good defense attorney would surely raise the issue of Jane Roe's lifestyle. While Coffee and Weddington privately felt that lifestyle and morality had nothing to do with the constitutionality of laws restricting abortion, they knew general public opinion held otherwise. Having a married couple join the case would dull defense efforts to focus on lifestyle.

The attorneys even considered dropping Jane Roe but quickly ruled out that action. Though the married woman previously had "suffered harm" because of the Texas antiabortion law, she was not pregnant at the time. It was not clear whether she would have legal standing in the suit. In legal terms, she lacked "a genuine case" where a "direct and significant effect" could result. A case involving her alone would likely be dismissed on that basis.

Two Separate Cases

After some discussion with legal experts well versed in constitutional matters, Weddington and Coffee decided to move forward with two separate cases, *Roe v. Wade* and *John and Mary Doe v. Wade*. While the two lawsuits generally attacked the same issues, filing them separately in different courts gave the lawyers two shots at getting a favorable hearing. Coffee's legal instincts told her the courts would most likely combine the cases, a common action when cases were so similar. Either way, a woman's right to obtain an abortion would make it to the federal level. Coffee filed the cases on March 3, 1970.

Coffee's instincts were right on target. A pretrial conference consolidated the two cases into one. The case, listed as *Roe v. Wade et al.*, was then assigned to a panel of three federal judges with expertise in matters involving interpretations of the Constitution. The three judges were no strangers to the spotlight. President Kennedy had appointed Judge Sarah Hughes to the bench in 1961. Much of the nation knew her as the judge who boarded Air Force One to swear in Lyndon Johnson as president following President Kennedy's assassination. Linda Coffee had

Protecting Jane Roe's Identity

Few legal issues are as emotionally charged as abortion. Sarah Weddington and Linda Coffee decided to protect their prospective plaintiff from the glare of the public eye by filing the lawsuit under a pseudonym, or false name. This tactic would allow the plaintiff to remain anonymous; no one except her attorneys would know her real name. It also protected the plaintiff from testifying in court or answering questions from opposing lawyers.

This was an important factor for Weddington and Coffee. They knew their plaintiff's background would meet with disapproval if it became public. It would be all too easy for questioning to emphasize personality and character. This would distract attention from what Weddington and Coffee believed were the real issues of the lawsuit: reproductive rights and a woman's right to choice regarding her own body. Their plaintiff chose to be known as Jane Roe.

By the time the Supreme Court finally issued its ruling in *Roe v. Wade,* nearly three years after the original decision in Dallas, the woman the world knew only as Jane Roe had settled into a new life as co-owner of a small business that cleaned offices. The American public's deeply divided and emotional response to the ruling astonished her, and she decided to reveal her true identity as Norma McCorvey. For the next twenty years, she worked vigorously to support abortion rights, answering telephone support lines and volunteering in abortion clinics.

That she became the "face" of abortion made McCorvey uncomfortable. Believing she had made the only choice she could at the time, she didn't understand why people reacted so strongly to her. She was neither savior nor Satan, and more painfully aware of her shortcomings than any of her critics. In her 1994 book, *I Am Roe— My Life, Roe v. Wade, and Freedom of Choice,* McCorvey wrote:

> I do not fit many people's idea of a historical role model. I am a rough woman, born into pain and anger and raised mostly by myself. I went to reform school, not high school or college. I have had many jobs but no professions. . . . They say that abortion is a controversial issue, but friends, let me tell you: privacy should not be controversial. It is a constitutional right. A human right. The movement didn't start with me. I was just the straw that broke the camel's back.

In the summer of 1995, McCorvey experienced a rebirth of faith and abruptly switched to support efforts to ban abortion. She has been active in antiabortion efforts since that time.

clerked for Judge Hughes, and held a deep respect for her objectivity and her interest in women's rights. Judge William Taylor had been a noted trial attorney before his appointment to the bench by President Johnson in 1966. Completing the triad was Dallas resident circuit court judge Irving Goldberg, admired among his peers for his quick wit and insightful probing and somewhat feared by the attorneys who faced him because he seldom left any aspect of an issue unexplored. Weddington and Coffee couldn't have gotten a more qualified panel if they had handpicked its members.

The Path to Trial

Attorneys for both sides began the task of preparing for trial much as opposing generals prepare for war. The plaintiffs attacked first. At the recommendation of attorneys with experience in constitutional matters, Weddington and Coffee executed what would turn out to be one of the most significant strategic moves in the case: They amended their filing to include class actions. Class action broadened the scope of the case to include any woman who, in the present or future, found herself prevented from obtaining an abortion because of the Texas statute.

It also prevented the court from dismissing the case on the grounds that Jane Roe's pregnancy was advanced beyond the remedy—a legal abortion—that the court could offer. This preemptive move was intended to thwart efforts by the defense to move for the case's dismissal on the basis of legal standing.

Written briefs presented the plaintiffs' reasons for believing

Sarah Hughes was one of the three judges who heard the 1970 case Roe v. Wade et al. *in Dallas, Texas.*

that Texas law was unconstitutional. In these complex legal documents, Weddington and Coffee emphasized what they felt were the legal precedents for overturning the law. These included earlier Supreme Court opinions that extended Fourth Amendment protection to assure the privacy of one's home and provided a definition of that privacy to include marital relations and matters of contraception.

Linda Coffee, a lawyer for the plaintiff in Roe v. Wade, *looks up from her desk while reviewing Texas law.*

As a last detail, Coffee and Weddington filed an affidavit, or written statement of testimony given under oath, about the circumstances of Jane Roe's pregnancy so that she would not have to testify in court. This formalized the anonymous filing to protect their client's privacy and prevented attorneys representing the state from knowing anything more about her. The less their opponents knew about Jane Roe's lifestyle, Weddington and Coffee felt, the more successfully they could keep the trial's focus on the issue of whether the state of Texas had the right to interfere with a woman's right to choose abortion.

Dallas County district attorney Henry Wade was named as the defendant in the case, as is the tradition in such lawsuits. It was Wade's responsibility to enforce Texas laws within his jurisdiction, and Jane Roe lived in Dallas. Wade was a diligent and respected attorney most widely known for prosecuting both Lee Harvey Oswald and Jack Ruby in the wake of President Kennedy's assassination. He believed the *Roe* case had little merit. Efforts to overturn abortion laws in numerous states, including this very same law in Texas, so far had been unsuccessful. Wade could see nothing unique or unusual about this one. He appointed one of his staff attorneys, John Tolle, to defend the suit.

Like his boss, Tolle did not see *Roe v. Wade* as fundamentally different from the dozens of other challenges to the Texas abortion statute. He prepared accordingly, focusing primarily on technical points of law. One such point was the issue of legal standing, as Weddington and Coffee anticipated. If Jane Roe was pregnant, she surely would not be by the time the case went to trial and thus could not obtain legal remedy—an abortion—through the court's decision. Tolle seemed unaware that Weddington and Coffee had amended their filing to make *Roe* a class action, making this issue moot (legally irrelevant). Tolle also challenged Jane Roe's legal standing on a different basis, that of legal harm. The Texas statute provided for prosecution of those who performed abortions, not those who obtained them. While the law made it illegal for Jane Roe to have an abortion, it could not punish her if she managed to do so.

Tolle built the remainder of his defense around the premise that the fetus, though unborn, was just as much a human being as the woman in whose womb it existed. As such, it had equal rights and protections under the Constitution and the laws of the

District Attorney Henry Wade, shown here in 1965, was already a respected prosecutor when he was called on to defend Texas law in the Roe v. Wade *case.*

country. To support this stance, Tolle researched court decisions that had awarded damages, albeit contingent upon live birth, to unborn fetuses injured in the womb. Medical articles and interviews with physicians further substantiated his perception that there was widespread belief in the medical field that the woman and the fetus were clearly separate entities. At the very least, Tolle felt, the evidence was strong enough to entitle both the fetus and the woman to the same rights. The court would unquestionably give the fetus's rights priority over the woman's, he believed, since to do otherwise would put the woman in control of the rights—and the life—of the fetus.

To counter the lawsuit's charge that the Texas law was vague, Tolle used the law's nearly one-hundred-year history as evidence that the opposite was in fact true. It had been challenged and upheld countless times. No law could survive so long, he argued, if its intent was unclear.

No case yet had defeated the impenetrable legal wall these combined arguments presented, and Tolle was confident that *Roe v. Wade* would be no exception. This confidence blinded Tolle to a crucial shift taking place in the nation's social environment, however. The women's movement was gaining momentum, even if it hadn't yet swept through Texas, and women's rights were a key issue. At some point the courts would be forced to decide whose rights prevailed. Weddington and Coffee hoped this case would be the one to push the point; it never occurred to Tolle that it could be.

Similar Defenses

The state of Texas also had an interest in defending the law. The state attorney general's office assigned attorney Jay Floyd to represent this interest and the state's position. Though Tolle and Floyd barely spoke to each other until the trial, they prepared surprisingly similar defenses. Floyd focused on the argument that the fetus was a separate being with rights of its own. He believed that aborting a two-month fetus was no different than murdering a two-month-old infant. He was confident that most people who opposed abortion shared this belief, and that most people opposed abortion. The moral wrongness of abortion, Floyd felt, would overcome any legal issues in how the Texas law was written. Floyd was so confident in this position that he considered his preparations complete and turned his attention to other matters until the trial.

The Trial Begins

At two o'clock in the afternoon on Friday, May 22, 1970, attorneys for the state of Texas and for the anonymous plaintiffs *Roe et al.* squared off before the three judges of the Fifth Circuit Court in Dallas. Outside the courthouse a handful of well-dressed, well-mannered picketers stood on the sidewalk displaying signs supporting a woman's right to freedom of choice. Spectators crowded the small courtroom, drawn by the issues yet unaware they were about to witness history in the making. The court's decision, no matter which side it favored, would reverberate through the entire nation.

Court procedures allotted equal time to each attorney who would address the court. Attorney Linda Coffee spoke first. She started a presentation to guide the judges through the case's highlights. Pretrial briefs filed about the case had emphasized the role of the Ninth Amendment, however, and the judges were eager to hear more about why the attorneys felt their case was based in the amendment's "unenumerated rights." They immediately interrupted with questions that refocused Coffee's discussion.

How was this amendment relevant to the case? What did unenumerated rights have to do with abortion? Why did Coffee believe abortion was a "fundamental freedom" on the same level as the constitutionally protected right to freedom of speech, press, assembly, and religion? Didn't the First, Fifth, and Fourteenth Amendments address such freedoms?

Startled but prepared, Coffee responded by affirming that yes, indeed, the First, Fifth, and Fourteenth Amendments were relevant and essential. The plaintiff believed the Texas law prohibiting abortion violated her right to due process, and to protection against state laws that restricted other constitutionally guaranteed rights. The case's key argument, however, was that abortion really was a right-to-privacy matter. While the right to privacy was not specifically stated, or enumerated, in the Constitution, numerous previous legal decisions had established and upheld its validity under the auspices of the Ninth Amendment. This case merely applied that right's definition to abortion. The comments satisfied the judges, who then allowed Coffee to present other aspects of the case.

When Sarah Weddington rose to present her arguments, she found her planned discussion similarly redirected by the judges. She had prepared to cite and discuss other cases in which judicial and legislative processes had determined that a fetus did not have the same legal rights as an individual had after birth. This would counter what she and Coffee expected as the state's defense. Instead, Weddington spent the rest of her allotted time responding to questions about the case's perceived constitutional issues.

A Direct and Intense Interrogation

Judge Goldberg was particularly intrigued with the arguments the *Roe* attorneys proposed. As Weddington expected from what she had heard of his approach, his interrogation was direct and intense. He instructed Weddington to assume that a Ninth Amendment right to protection of privacy did exist "and address the question of whether the state has any compelling interests in regulating abortion." Weddington acknowledged that the state could have justification for establishing narrowly drawn regulations that would, for example, prohibit those who were not licensed physicians from performing abortions just as they were prohibited from performing any other medical or surgical procedure. States routinely restricted the practice of medicine to those who were properly trained and licensed, and Weddington saw no reason to challenge their authority or appropriateness to do so.

Judge Goldberg pressed Weddington to consider the various dimensions of abortion. Was there sufficient justification to require all abortions be done in a hospital? Should there be different standards for married and single women? Neither had justification nor would serve any compelling state interest, came Weddington's response.

Then it was the defense's turn. Jay Floyd, the first of the two attorneys representing the state of Texas to speak, opened the state's presentation by challenging Jane Roe's legal standing, which he asserted was lacking. This argument gave the impression that Floyd was as unaware of the case's amended class-action status as his cocounsel was. Floyd argued that the case was moot, or without legal merit, because the unknown Jane Roe was either too far along in her pregnancy or had already given birth, meaning she could not obtain remedy even if the court decided in her favor. Floyd suggested that the court dismiss Jane Roe's claim.

Less Than Impressed

Judge Goldberg was less than impressed with Floyd's opening remarks. He questioned Floyd about the suit's class-action status. Apparently unknown to Floyd, Judge Goldberg had played pivotal roles in several landmark class-action decisions including the famous public school desegregation case *Brown v. Board of Education*. Floyd misunderstood Judge Goldberg's sarcastic tone. He countered with what Judge Goldberg perceived to be a somewhat flippant response, persisting in the view that Roe's legal standing remained questionable because she would not personally benefit from a ruling in her favor. Irritated, Judge Goldberg chided Floyd for his narrow view and lectured him about the scope of class actions. The exchange rattled Floyd, and it took him a few minutes to regain his composure.

The judge pressed on to his topic of interest. He directed Floyd to address the topic of vagueness as it was relevant to the Ninth Amendment. Floyd was not prepared to respond. The state's position hinged on the belief that the fetus was a distinct being, and as such was entitled to the same protections under law as any other individual. He had prepared arguments to support only this contention.

Struggling to turn the direction back to the arguments he wanted to present, Floyd started his response by discussing the state's interest in protecting the fetus. This interest, he argued, extended to the point of conception because this was the point the state established as the beginning of life. Judge Goldberg pressed Floyd to explain how the state had established this extension, given that scientists and medical professionals had not yet been able to do so. Floyd agreed that there were controversies and disagreements regarding such an extension. Now completely flustered, he attempted to support his position by citing a California case that he remembered. Floyd realized too late that the case had resulted in a ruling that abortion was a matter of privacy between a woman and her physician. He spent the remaining minutes of his allotted time attempting to recover, but the effort was futile.

The trial's final arguments belonged to John Tolle, who was left with the unenviable task of resuscitating a critically wounded defense. Abandoning his planned comments, Tolle shifted into damage control mode. He started by agreeing with many of the points Weddington and Coffee made. The issue, he said, was not when life began but who had the right to establish an "arbitrary time" from a legal perspective. Such a right belonged to the states, he argued.

As he had done with the other attorneys, Judge Goldberg questioned Tolle about the Texas law's constitutionality. Tolle reasserted the defense's position that the law was constitutional as it was written. The state did not believe, he said, that the law infringed on the rights of women. Rather, it protected the rights of the unborn fetus. A law prohibiting abortion, he held, was simply a matter of the state exercising its authority, and need, to moderate conflicting rights.

In this circumstance, Tolle asserted, Texas had not only a right but also an obligation to protect the rights

Sarah Weddington found her planned argument redirected by Judge Goldberg's questions.

THIRD PLAINTIFF JOINS SUIT

As they prepared for trial, Weddington and Coffee knew their case had some weaknesses. The anonymity of Jane Roe withstood the first challenge from the defense when Judge Sarah Hughes over-ruled a defense petition to question the plaintiff in person. However, the court was likely to honor the defense's request to dismiss the Does as plaintiffs on the basis of legal standing. Mary Doe was not pregnant and, because of her medical condition, was not likely to become pregnant. Without her, the defense could more narrowly limit testimony to the legal aspects of the issue.

Shortly before the case was scheduled to go to trial, the lawyers for physician James H. Hallford asked to add their client to *Roe*. Hallford had been charged with violating the Texas law for performing abor-tions. His attorneys felt his case would lend further credibility to the medical aspects of abortion. In particular, the physician could credi-bly establish abortion as a medical procedure and the decision to obtain one as a medical matter between a patient and her physician.

Though concerned that the doctor's pending criminal charges could affect the judges' perceptions of his testimony, Weddington and Cof-fee decided that Hallford's potential contributions outweighed any concerns about his legal status. His participation also would give the case standing on the basis of legal harm. They welcomed the addi-tion to their case.

Hallford's attorneys conducted the preparations and trial presenta-tion for their client. The Dallas court's ruling determined that the Texas law against abortion violated a woman's right to privacy as pro-tected by the Ninth Amendment. It also found the law to be uncon-stitutionally vague, citing the Fourteenth Amendment. This vagueness failed to provide adequate guidelines for physicians, the judges said. The court's failure to follow the ruling with an injunc-tion to prevent prosecution of those who violated the law, however, meant that the Dallas district attorney's office could move ahead to prosecute Hallford, which it did. Prosecutors finally dropped the two criminal indictments against Hallford when the U.S. Supreme Court issued its *Roe v. Wade* ruling.

---

of the fetus over the rights of the mother. His concluding com-ments reflected the underlying belief of the state's attorneys that no court would ever reverse these priorities.

> I think that the most persuasive right that the plaintiffs urge . . . is the right to privacy, for want of a better term, and there you get to the point where the state has to regulate

conflicting rights, whether the state has got an interest in the life of the unborn child sufficient to regulate the woman's right to privacy. This is a very difficult question . . . I personally think, and I think the state's position will be, and is, that the right of the child to life is superior to that of the woman's right to privacy.

A Confusing Ruling

Less than a month later, on June 17, 1970, the Fifth Circuit Court issued its decision on *Roe v. Wade*. In a brief, thirteen-page ruling, the court found the Texas law prohibiting abortion unconstitutional. The court agreed with the plaintiff's contention that the Ninth Amendment did safeguard women's right to privacy. A woman's choice to have children was an exercise of that right. In their ruling, the judges wrote:

> Freedom to choose in the matter of abortions has been accorded the status of a "fundamental" right in every case [the court knew about]. The burden is on the defendant to demonstrate to the satisfaction of the Court that the infringement [by Texas laws prohibiting abortion] is necessary to support a compelling state interest. The defendant has failed to meet this burden.

> On the merits, plaintiffs argue as their principal contention that the Texas abortion laws must be declared unconstitutional because they deprive single women and married couples of their right, secured by the Ninth Amendment, to choose whether to have children. We agree.

Despite its strong assertions, the ruling did not include an injunction against the state of Texas to prevent it from continuing to prosecute cases under the law the judges determined was unconstitutional. This oversight, whether intentional or not, surprised both sides. It seemed a point of detail so obvious as to be silly, yet without an instruction specifically enjoining the state of Texas from continuing to enforce its illegal law it appeared that the state could still prosecute violators.

Dallas district attorney Henry Wade saw a partial victory in the confusing ruling. He announced that the state fully intended to continue prosecuting violations of the law since the court had not specifically said it could not. "Apparently we're free to try them, so we'll still do so," he said.

At first disappointed, the *Roe* attorneys quickly realized the puzzling omission was an open door to a direct U.S. Supreme Court appeal. This was what they wanted all along—an opportunity to force the issue on a national level, to obtain a ruling that would affect abortion laws in all states. A little case in Texas was suddenly the flashpoint for women's rights nationwide.

Chapter 2

The Road to
Roe v. Wade

THOUGH *ROE V. WADE* UNSETTLED a nation overnight, the case was nearly a hundred years in the making. *Roe* was the cumulative result of hundreds of restrictive laws and the suits that challenged them. Many of these laws were based on two far-reaching pieces of legislation passed in the 1870s, the Comstock Law and the Barnum Law. Both outlawed not just abortion but birth control practices other than abstinence. Many of the lawsuits that challenged these and similar laws attempted to ease restrictions on birth control, not necessarily legalize abortion.

A History of Controversy

There is historical evidence that abortion was widely accepted and practiced in ancient cultures for several thousand years as a means of birth and population control, long before there were methods other than abstinence to prevent conception. The practice began to fall from favor in the thirteenth century. Abortion eventually became a crime under common law in Western cultures that considered it murder, not contraception. Until the eighteenth century, guilt was punishable by hanging. By the 1700s, common law dealing with abortion had evolved to two levels divided by quickening, or the point at which a woman feels movement (generally between the fourth and fifth months). Prequickening abortions were misdemeanor offenses. Abortions after quickening were felony offenses that carried stiff punishment, sometimes even death. Both the women who obtained abortions and the individuals who assisted them were subject to prosecution under most such laws.

Like many other tenets of common law, the abortion prohibition carried over into statutory criminal law when the United States began codifying, or formalizing, its laws. Connecticut was the first state to enact legislation making abortion a crime, which it did in 1821. Other states soon followed suit, and by the 1860s abortion was illegal throughout America. Legal scholars and medical historians believe these controls on abortion had less to do with morality than with regulation of the medical profession, which was still loosely defined at that time. It did not take long for that balance to shift, however. Most statutory abortion laws punished the person who performed the abortion rather than the woman who obtained it.

The Comstock Law: "Instruments of an Immoral Nature"

During America's first century as an independent country, large families were desirable. More children meant more hands to do chores and manage the activities of daily living that were necessary to survive. Women "belonged" to the men in their lives—first their fathers, then their husbands. Contraceptive methods, even when desired, were severely limited.

By the 1870s, matters of reproduction became intermingled with issues of morality. Responding to pressure from church groups and citizens alike, states and finally the federal government passed laws to "restore virtue." In 1873 President Ulysses S. Grant signed into law the *Act for the Suppression of Trade in and Circulation of Obscene Literature*

Anthony Comstock was the driving force behind the so-called Comstock Law, passed in 1873, which outlawed abortion.

and Articles of Immoral Use, nicknamed the Comstock Law after its most ardent and outspoken supporter, Anthony Comstock.

The long arm of the Comstock Law reached broadly and deeply into private lives. The law made it a federal crime, punishable by fines and prison time, to publish, sell, buy, or possess material defined by very narrow standards as obscene. The law also made it illegal for anyone to use, sell, or advertise any "instrument or other article of an immoral nature, or any drug or medicine, or any article whatever, for the prevention of conception, or for causing unlawful abortion." The Comstock Law resulted in the arrests, convictions, and prison sentences of thousands of people during the forty years Anthony Comstock served as its chief enforcer.

The federal law remained active and enforceable until President Richard Nixon signed into law the legislation repealing it on January 8, 1971, only six months after the Fifth Circuit Court of Appeals issued its ruling in *Roe v. Wade.*

The Barnum Law: "The Wickedness of Humankind"

The Comstock Law inspired a successful Connecticut businessman to use it as a model to further reduce the "wickedness of humankind" in his home state. Better known for his role as America's circus showman, Phineas T. Barnum was also an active politician. From his positions as mayor of Bridgeport, Connecticut, and as a representative elected to the Connecticut General Assembly, he launched what ultimately became the country's most restrictive anti–birth control law.

Passed into law in 1879, the public act known as the Barnum Law outlawed any method of birth control except abstinence, even among married couples. Under the Barnum Law, it was a criminal offense for any woman to possess, and any doctor to prescribe, any form of birth control. The Barnum Law remained in effect and was enforced until its overturn in 1965.

"The Right to Be Let Alone"

In the early decades of the twentieth century, individual rights remained narrowly defined. Cases challenging such narrow interpretations were routinely defeated. Though not about the issue of abortion, several of these cases became important influences in *Roe v. Wade*.

The first of these was 1928's *Olmstead v. United States*, in which the U.S. Supreme Court let stand a lower court decision finding the defendant Roy Olmstead guilty of illegally transporting alcohol on the basis of evidence obtained through wiretapping. *Olmstead* argued that the wiretapping was illegal under the protections of the Fourth Amendment. The Court disagreed. In its limited interpretation, the Court held that the Fourth Amendment protected only an individual's material effects, not intangibles such as voice transmissions. (The Court reversed itself six years later, after passage of the Federal Communications Act prohibiting the interception of any communications.)

Of far greater significance than the case's outcome was the dissenting opinion of Justice Louis Brandeis, who strongly disagreed with the majority opinion to uphold Olmstead's conviction. In his passionate dissent, Brandeis eloquently articulated what soon became known as the "right to be let alone." In criticizing his colleagues' narrow interpretation of the Fourth Amendment, Brandeis wrote:

> The protection guaranteed by the Amendments is much broader in scope. The makers of our Constitution undertook to secure conditions favorable to the pursuit of happiness. They recognized the significance of man's spiritual nature, or his feelings, and of his intellect. They knew that only a part of the pain, pleasure and satisfactions of life are to be found in material things. They sought to protect Americans in their beliefs, their thoughts, their emotions and their sensations. They conferred, as against the Government, the right to be let alone—the most comprehensive of rights, and the right most valued by civilized men. To protect that right, every unjustifiable intrusion by the Government upon the privacy of the individual, whatever the means employed, must be deemed a violation of the Fourth Amendment. And the use, as evidence in a criminal proceeding, of facts

ascertained by such intrusion must be deemed a violation of the Fifth.

Though Justice Brandeis's words did little to influence his judicial colleagues in *Olmstead v. United States*, they gave birth to a concept that would come of age nearly forty years later.

Decisions About Personal Privacy

By the 1960s, personal and civil liberties took center stage in judicial decisions as the nation's focus shifted to individual rights. Other cases began to draw from and expand upon Justice Brandeis's "right to be let alone" premise. One such case that did so successfully was *Mapp v. Ohio* in 1961. In this case, police broke into the home of Dolly Mapp on a tip that a suspect was hiding there. The search turned up no sign of the suspect, though police did seize printed materials considered obscene. Since possession of obscene materials was a criminal offense, the police arrested Mapp. She was subsequently convicted. The appeal to the U.S. Supreme Court argued that the search was illegal because it violated Mapp's Fourth Amendment rights.

This time the Court agreed with such an argument, using the "right to be let alone" as the foundation for its ruling that the Fourth Amendment assures the privacy of an individual's home. This established the concept of personal privacy as a protected, though unspecified, constitutional guarantee. While the Court's ruling in *Mapp* is better known for

According to Supreme Court Justice Louis Brandeis, "every unjustifiable intrusion by the Government upon the privacy of the individual" is a violation of the Fourth Amendment.

what law enforcement officials call the exclusionary rule, which prevents prosecutors from using evidence seized in illegal searches, this concept was critical to *Roe v. Wade*.

Less successful was *Poe v. Ullman*'s attempt in the same year to extend the premise of the "right to be let alone" to the personal relationship between a husband and wife in a challenge to the Barnum Law. The case contested the state law's authority to regulate birth control practices between married couples. A key argument presented by *Poe* attorney Fowler Harper invoked the Ninth Amendment's unenumerated rights, emphasizing that privacy was one such right. Harper argued that the Barnum Law overstepped the boundaries of this right when its enforcement resulted in the arrest of married couples for activities that took place within the privacy of their homes.

> When the long arm of the law reaches into the bedroom and regulates the most sacred relations between a man and his wife, it is going too far. There must be a limit to the extent to which the moral scruples of a minority, or for that matter a majority, can be enacted into laws which regulate the sex life of all married people. . . . The normal and voluntary relations of spouses in the privacy of their homes is regarded as beyond the prying eyes of peeping toms, be they police officers or legislators.

> [The plaintiffs] complain that it is precisely their privacy in their homes and, indeed, in the most private part thereof that is invaded. They want to be let alone in the bedroom. They insist that marital intercourse may not be rationed, censored or regulated by priest, legislator or bureaucrat. Certainly, they contend, the "liberty" guaranteed by the due process clause includes this, among the most sacred experiences of life.

The argument failed to convince the Court, which dismissed *Poe v. Ullman* on a 5-4 decision finding that the plaintiffs had not demonstrated any real threat of prosecution. Once again, however, a dissenting opinion that invoked the "right to be let alone" drew considerable attention in legal circles. Justice John Marshall Harlan's dissent was three times as long as the majority opinion in the case. He argued that Connecticut's Barnum Law violated both the Fourth and Fourteenth Amendments. While the right to privacy is not an absolute, Harlan acknowledged,

> The intimacy of husband and wife is necessarily an essential and accepted feature of the institution of marriage, an institution which the State not only must allow, but which always and in every age it has fostered and protected. It is one thing when the State exerts its power either to forbid extramarital sexuality altogether, or to say who may marry, but it is quite another when, having acknowledged a marriage and the intimacies inherent in it, it undertakes to regulate by means of the criminal law the details of that intimacy. [The appellants] have presented a very pressing claim for constitutional protection against the utter novelty of [Connecticut's] obnoxiously intrusive statute.

The Penumbra Doctrine: "Between the Lines"

Harlan's words were eerily prophetic. Less than four years later, the Court again faced the issue of the right to personal privacy in *Griswold v. Connecticut*. To force another challenge of the Barnum Law, Connecticut Planned Parenthood's executive director Estelle Griswold and prominent physician Lee Buxton, who served as the agency's medical director, opened a birth control clinic. They then made sure the police knew of their operation. Under the auspices of the Barnum Law, the police promptly arrested the pair and closed the clinic. As they expected, the local court convicted them. This cleared the way for the appeal to the Supreme Court that Griswold and Buxton hoped would put an end to what they felt were unconstitutional intrusions into private lives.

This time the Court ruled 7-2 that the Barnum Law did in fact violate the right to privacy implied by the Ninth Amendment. Justice William O. Douglas, who also had dissented on *Poe*

Estelle Griswold (second from left) and Lee Buxton (second from right) are shown here during their 1961 trial in Connecticut. Their conviction allowed them to appeal to the Supreme Court.

(though not as eloquently as his colleague Justice Harlan), wrote the majority opinion. He established the interpretation that key rights existed "between the lines" of the enumerated, or written, rights defined within the Constitution. In the opinion that later became known as the penumbra, or shadow, doctrine, Justice Douglas elaborated on this critical interpretation.

> Specific guarantees in the Bill of Rights have penumbras, formed by emanations from those guarantees that help give them life and substance. Various guarantees create zones of privacy. The right of association contained in the penumbra of the First Amendment is one, as we have seen. The Third Amendment, in its prohibition against the quartering of soldiers "in any house" in time of peace without the consent of the owner, is another facet of that privacy. The Fourth Amendment explicitly affirms "the right of the people to be secure in their persons, houses, papers, and effects, against unreasonable searches and seizures." The Fifth Amendment,

in its Self-Incrimination Clause, enables the citizen to create a zone of privacy which government may not force him to surrender to his detriment. The Ninth Amendment provides: "The enumeration in the Constitution, of certain rights, shall not be construed to deny or disparage others retained by the people."

Consequently, Justice Douglas concluded, "the present case, then, concerns a relationship lying within the zone of privacy created by several fundamental constitutional guarantees."

With this finding, the Court ruled that Connecticut's Barnum Law amounted to unreasonable intrusion into marital privacy in violation of various elements of the First, Third, Fourth, Fifth, and Ninth Amendments. The ruling overturned the convictions of Estelle Griswold and Lee Buxton, and effectively ended the Barnum Law's reign.

Other Legal Challenges

The Court's decision in *Griswold* affected laws only in Connecticut. While the ruling struck down the Barnum Law's intrusive reach into the private practices of married couples, it did not specifically permit abortion. Nor did the ruling affect similar laws in other states. Pressing the point that abortion was a form of contraception and as such was a decision protected by a woman's right to privacy, other legal challenges began to take on these laws. One key case was *United States v. Vuitch*, a 1971 case in which the District of Columbia attempted to prosecute physician Milan Vuitch for performing abortions. Even as *Griswold* supporters were gearing up for an appeal, U.S. district judge Gerhard Gesell issued a surprise decision dismissing criminal charges against Vuitch on the grounds that the D.C. law was unconstitutionally vague. The law, which had remained unchanged since its enactment in 1901, permitted abortions "necessary for the preservation of the mother's life or health." This, according to Judge Gesell, provided no clear standard for physicians to follow, failing "to give that certainty which due process of law considers essential in a criminal statute."

In his written opinion, Judge Gesell also noted a changing attitude evident in the Supreme Court's decisions to support the view that

> As a secular matter a woman's liberty and right of privacy extends to family, marriages and sex matters and may well include the right to remove an unwanted child at least in the early stages of pregnancy. . . . The asserted constitutional right of privacy, here the unqualified right to refuse to bear children, has limitations. Congress can undoubtedly regulate abortion practice in many ways, perhaps even establishing different standards at various phases of pregnancy.

The Supreme Court overturned the reasoning of Judge Gesell's ruling six months later. While the Court left intact the lower court's dismissal of the charges against Vuitch, it found that the law provided sufficient standards for physicians to know whether they were in compliance. The D.C. law's use of the term *health* was in fact adequately broad, wrote Justice Hugo Black in the majority decision, as long as it was understood to include "psychological as well as physical well-being." Justice Potter Stewart concurred, elaborating that this meant

> When a physician has exercised his judgment in favor of performing an abortion, he has, by hypothesis, not violated

In 1971, Judge Gerhard Gesell (pictured) dismissed criminal charges against Milan Vuitch for performing abortions.

ROE V. WADE's EFFECT ON ABORTION RATES

Before *Roe v. Wade* overturned state laws that prohibited abortion, legalized abortions were hard to come by in the United States. A handful of states allowed abortion under restricted conditions but most outlawed it.

As expected, the number of legalized abortions performed throughout the United States skyrocketed after *Roe v. Wade* removed state prohibitions against them. In 1972, there were fewer than 500,000 legal abortions performed nationwide (though there is no way to know how many women obtained illegal abortions). Four years later, the figure had nearly doubled to more than 980,000. The number of legal abortions rose to a high of 1.4 million in 1990, then began a steady decline.

Women who choose abortion usually have more than one reason for doing so. Most did not expect the pregnancy, and often find its timing inconvenient—they are in school, building careers, or have other demanding responsibilities. Many are either single or involved in uncertain relationships. Economic issues almost always play a role.

Analysts attribute the downward trend in abortions to multiple influences. Improved education and methods have increased the use of birth control to prevent unwanted pregnancies. Aggressive anti-abortion efforts have influenced some women to seek alternatives such as adoption. In addition, abortion services are not available in all locations, and they are particularly scarce in rural areas.

Another significant influence, social analysts believe, is the changing social acceptance of unwed mothers. The percentage of single women giving birth has risen as well, from just over 10 percent in 1970 to nearly 30 percent in 1990.

the statute. I think the question of whether the performance of an abortion is "necessary for the preservation of the mother's life or health" is entrusted under the statute exclusively to those licensed to practice medicine. . . . [Any physician] would be wholly immune from being charged with the commission of a criminal offense under this law.

Justice Douglas dissented. He disagreed with Justice Black that the only merits under consideration in *Vuitch* were those relating to the issue of vagueness. In his dissenting opinion, Justice Douglas returned to the themes of the majority decision he crafted in *Griswold*. "Abortion touches quite intimate affairs of the family, of marriage, of sex, which in *Griswold* . . . we held to involve rights associated with several express constitutional rights and which are summed up in the right of privacy." Under no circumstances, Justice Douglas felt, did the government have the authority to inject itself into those affairs or those rights.

The last case to have significant bearing before the Court's landmark ruling in *Roe v. Wade* was *Eisenstadt v. Baird*. Bill Baird had been convicted in 1967 of violating a Massachusetts law prohibiting anyone other than a nurse, doctor, or pharmacist from distributing contraceptives. Baird frequently lectured about birth control, and he routinely handed out samples of contraceptives following his lectures. Baird's sentence of jail time was stayed while he appealed his case to the Supreme Court.

The Court overturned Baird's conviction. In writing the majority opinion, Justice William Brennan took *Griswold* even further by extending the concept of "marital privacy" to individual privacy.

A 1967 photo shows Bill Baird being led from Boston University following his arrest for distributing contraceptives to students.

NONSURGICAL METHODS MAY TRULY MAKE ABORTION A PRIVATE MATTER

When *Roe v. Wade* made history in 1973, surgery was the only abortion option. It wasn't possible to detect pregnancy much earlier than eight weeks, by which time the fetus was well implanted in the uterus. Abortion techniques involved either scraping the walls of the uterus or removing the fetus with a powerful suction machine. The risks were those of any other surgery—infection and excessive bleeding.

Since then, medical advances have made it possible to detect pregnancy much earlier and more privately. Home pregnancy tests are easily available and can identify pregnancy with reasonable accuracy as early as a few weeks following conception. More sophisticated tests, such as blood hormone levels and pelvic ultrasound, can detect pregnancy even sooner. With early detection and new medical techniques, physicians can also perform abortions much earlier in pregnancy, which reduces the potential for medical complications.

Without the risks of surgery, there is no need for women to go to hospitals or surgical clinics for abortions. Only the woman and her doctor need know. A physician can use a hand-held syringe guided by an ultrasound (images formed by bouncing sound waves through the abdomen) to perform an abortion right in the office as soon as one week after conception, with no greater risk than a pelvic examination.

A woman who has had unprotected sex can also ask her physician for "morning after" pills, drugs that prevent the body from releasing the hormones necessary to make pregnancy possible. When taken within seventy-two hours of intercourse, such drugs can prevent a fertilized egg from implanting in the uterus. They cause the uterus to shed its lining as it does during menstruation, resulting in what seems to the woman like a moderately heavy menstrual flow. If more than seventy-two hours but less than seven days have passed since the unprotected intercourse, the physician can insert an intrauterine device, or IUD, to prevent the fertilized egg from implanting.

Justice Brennan asserted that limiting the right to privacy to couples violated the Constitution's equal protection clause by discriminating against unmarried individuals. In his remarks, he wrote:

> If the right of privacy means anything, it is the right of the individual, married or single, to be free from unwarranted government intrusion into matters so fundamentally affecting a person as the decision whether to bear or beget a child.

Legal analysts immediately interpreted Justice Brennan's remarks as setting the stage for *Roe v. Wade*, on which the Court had already heard appeals.

Ready for *Roe v. Wade*

There was no single precedent case that prepared the way for *Roe v. Wade*. Hundreds of cases challenged state and federal laws restricting contraception and prohibiting abortion; only a handful made it to the Supreme Court. Though history books credit these few cases with advancing the cause of individual rights, in reality the process was painstakingly tedious. Like the playwright who becomes an overnight success after the script he has worked on for twenty years is finally produced, *Roe v. Wade* represents the cumulative results of all the cases that went before it.

Chapter 3

Preparing for the High Court

SINCE THEIR INTEREST IN overturning abortion laws had united them in the late 1960s, Sarah Weddington and Linda Coffee had watched others mount countless court challenges attacking the constitutionality of issues suddenly seen within the new context of individual rights. Some, like *Griswold v. Connecticut*, *United States v. Vuitch*, and *Eisenstadt v. Baird*, seemed to support the more liberal social climate by granting limited freedom to make choices about birth control. Courts at all levels upheld many others.

The two *Roe* attorneys knew that the key to how their case would fare before the justices of the U.S. Supreme Court rested in the preparations that had started with their early decisions about how to frame and present the case in federal district court. These decisions established the framework from within which the Court would evaluate the case's arguments. Some of the more critical of these decisions included amending the filing to class-action status, adding Dr. Hallford as a plaintiff, and focusing on the Ninth Amendment as the source of constitutional protection of a woman's right to privacy and to abortion as an exercise of that right.

The Road to the Supreme Court

The American judicial system allows most court decisions to be appealed, or reconsidered by a different court. Generally, cases heard in federal district courts are appealed to a court of appeals,

47

Abortion opponents (shown rallying here) and supporters realized the significance of the Roe v. Wade *case as it wound its way to the Supreme Court.*

often called an appellate court. Under certain circumstances a case can be appealed directly to the Supreme Court. One such circumstance—the federal district court fails to grant requested injunctive relief (an order to stop prosecuting violators of the law)—applied in *Roe v. Wade.*

As the final stop in the American judicial system, the Supreme Court hears only appeals. It is not obligated to hear all the appeals presented to it. In fact, it hears only 150 or so of the thousands it receives each year, almost exclusively focusing on those that raise issues of constitutionality. Supreme Court opinions are significant not just because they provide a final decision in a particular case but because they often redefine the law the case challenges. Court opinions do not themselves become law; they return the task of recrafting the law to the state legislature that originally passed it.

A Supreme Court determination that a particular state law is unconstitutional also applies to similar laws in other states. A favorable ruling for *Roe* would effectively end abortion laws as they currently existed not only in Texas but in every state. On the other hand, a ruling affirming the Texas law would virtually guarantee that abortion laws would remain unchanged until another means of challenging them surfaced.

Attorneys who want the Supreme Court to review lower court decisions they feel are wrong must first file a notice of appeal with the Court. They then have sixty days to craft a written explanation presenting the reasons the Court should accept the case. A New York attorney specializing in constitutional law, Roy Lucas, stepped forward to offer the *Roe* attorneys his help in preparing this explanation. His James Madison Constitutional Law Institute had been involved in a number of abortion cases throughout the country, one of the most prominent being *United States v. Vuitch*. Novices in both constitutional law and Supreme Court appeals, Weddington and Coffee gladly accepted.

Of the nine justices who ordinarily sit on the Court, four must agree to hear the case. On May 21, 1971, the U.S. Supreme Court agreed to hear *Roe v. Wade* and another abortion law case from Georgia, *Doe v. Bolton*, at an as yet to be determined date in October. Legal analysts speculated that the Court selected the cases because they represented different aspects of the abortion issue, providing a broad basis for considering the constitutional arguments at the heart of the abortion debate.

Briefs and Documents

Once the Court agreed to hear the case, the attorneys for each side prepared the legal documents, or briefs, the justices would review before hearing oral arguments. Briefs were typically complex and full of legal technicalities, often citing previous case decisions the attorneys hoped would influence the justices. Each side's brief could be only 150 pages long. Because of this limitation, it was a common strategy for each side to use its brief to summarize the case's major points and then ask others to submit amici curiae, or "friends of the courts," briefs that elaborated on these points. Typically, amici briefs came from organizations with an interest in the issues of the case. Forty-two groups responded on behalf of *Roe*, including the American Civil Liberties Union, the Association for the Study of Abortion, Planned Parenthood, the American College of Obstetricians and Gynecologists, and the family law section of the American Bar Association.

It was critical that there be no technical errors in the briefs, and no administrative errors in their preparation and filing with the Court. Either could result in the Court refusing to accept the case, and there was no second chance. It was also important for the briefs to be comprehensive and to present the case's key points in a clear, logical manner. Unlike a regular trial, Supreme Court proceedings did not allow any witnesses to testify. Only the lawyers representing each side were permitted to speak. They were limited in time, which they typically spent answering questions the justices had after reading the briefs. Oral arguments, no matter how persuasive, could seldom overcome the damaging effects of poorly written briefs.

The *Roe* team also had to provide copies of the 139-page record containing all the previously submitted documents as well as transcripts of the lower court's hearing and decision.

The Supreme Court in 1970 (from left to right): John Marshall Harlan, Thurgood Marshall, Hugo Black, Potter Stewart, Warren Burger, Byron White, William Douglas, Harry Blackmun, and William Brennan.

Finally, the *Roe* brief included a nearly 500-page appendix containing reference and support documents.

None of the *Roe* lawyers really had the time to dedicate to the demanding process. Coffee's law firm required her services full-time and then some to manage the caseload that had accumulated while she had worked on the earlier aspects of *Roe v. Wade*. Weddington was working as an assistant city attorney in Fort Worth, Texas, giving as much time as she could beyond her job to efforts to change Texas abortion laws. Again Roy Lucas came to the rescue. He offered Weddington a part-time job at his institute in New York so she would have an opportunity to prepare the appeal. Realizing she needed both the income and Lucas's expertise, Weddington accepted.

In addition to taking the lead in preparing the *Roe* brief, Lucas had agreed to prepare an amicus brief for the *Doe v. Bolton* hearing. His workload overflowed. Despite the impressive name of his institute and his title as its president, Lucas was its only full-time attorney. He worked long hours aided only by law students. When Weddington joined him, she found her part-time job occupied all of her time. Lucas filed for one, then a second, extension of the deadline for submitting the briefs.

Desperate for Help

By the time Lucas and Weddington finally got started on the *Roe v. Wade* brief, they were desperate for help. They drafted several attorneys who were knowledgeable of Supreme Court procedures or had an interest in the abortion issue. By the time it was completed, their 145-page document carried the names of seven attorneys.

The first half of the brief focused on abortion as a health decision between a woman and her physician. To establish this point, its authors presented pages and pages of technical documentation about the medical aspects and procedures of abortion. The *Roe* team placed this section first because it seemed the most essential to the argument that a woman's right to choose abortion was a private decision between her and her physician. Another portion of the brief focused on an issue that would later take on greater prominence. While the Constitution assured its protection to "all persons born or naturalized in the United States," the brief noted, there had not as yet been any cases extending this to an unborn fetus. The team scrambled to file the brief by the deadline.

Texas Defends Its Abortion Law

Meanwhile, the Texas attorney general's office was busy in Dallas preparing its defense of the lower court decision and the state's abortion law. Assistant attorney general Jay Floyd, who had handled the district court case, was in the lead. While his staff had a month longer to prepare its briefs so that it could respond to the *Roe* briefs, Floyd's staff was equally overburdened with other work. As had happened with the *Roe* team, his rescue came from an outside source. Two Chicago attorneys, Dennis Horan and Jerome Frazel, were already preparing an amicus brief defending the Texas law. They offered their assistance in preparing the appeals brief, too, an offer a grateful Floyd accepted.

Like their *Roe* counterparts, the Chicago pair spent the major portion of their appeals brief discussing the medical issues of abortion. They focused on the procedure's risks and complications, however, and included ten graphic photos of aborted fetuses. Floyd inserted the material the two sent just as they wrote it, then crafted his own lead to introduce it. Though at the time of the trial in Dallas, Floyd had relied heavily on the presentation of the fetus as a human being with its own set of rights, he didn't have a strong personal conviction about it one way or the other. However, by the time he finished his research for the appeals brief, composed in large part of the materials sent by the two Chicago attorneys, he unequivocally accepted this view.

"The right to life of the unborn child is superior to the right of privacy of the mother," Floyd argued. He used considerable space in the brief supporting this view with substantial medical evidence bolstered by moral concerns. The position drew strong support among those who filed amici briefs and became a key point that Floyd would press in his oral arguments before the

COULD A BETTER PREPARED TEXAS HAVE CHANGED THE OUTCOME?

The time constraints that led Jay Floyd to use verbatim the material from the Chicago attorneys who stepped in to help prepare the state of Texas's brief would later haunt the case. After the Court's historic ruling overturning the Texas court's decision, legal critics dissecting the case noted that the state's brief and the amicus brief Horan and Frazel also prepared contained nearly half the same content and all of the same photos.

Much of the Texas brief simply repeated the positions the state had argued in its district court appearance. Since the Court already had transcripts of the original trial, this presentation in the Texas brief was a repetition for which the busy Court had little patience. Floyd's newfound fervor about the position that the fetus's right to life outweighed the mother's right to privacy was old news to the Court; it had been the basis of Dallas assistant district attorney John Tolle's argument. And despite the clear evidence that the *Roe* attorneys would continue pressing the issues of unenumerated rights and the penumbra concept, the Texas brief failed to address these crucial points.

Other mistakes slipped through. Legal analysts pointed out numerous grammar and punctuation errors that sometimes made key points difficult to understand or even altered their meanings. Misspelled names in cited judicial references, mistakes for which the Court had a notable intolerance, threatened the entire brief on points of technicality.

Despite the flaws in his brief, however, Floyd did a commendable job given that the state of Texas provided him with very little assistance beyond clerical support. Neither Dallas County district attorney Henry Wade nor his assistant attorney who had represented the state's interest in the district court trial, John Tolle, participated in preparing the state's appeal brief. Wade acknowledged some years after the Court's ruling that he really had no interest in the case, did not read the decision, and was himself ambivalent about abortion. He felt that in some cases abortion was justified, and as far as the decision was concerned, he didn't "really have any views on it, either way."

To many observers and analysts, it appeared that once again the state of Texas defeated itself through inadequate preparation and failing to take seriously the far-reaching ramifications of the high court's decision. Though a well-written brief would not by itself win a Court decision, a poorly prepared brief risked losing one. There was considerable speculation that a stronger appeals brief by the Texas attorneys could have directed a different outcome.

Court. Floyd also incorporated into his introductory remarks the key finding from *Griswold* asserting that the "prevention of abortion does not entail state interference with the right of marital intercourse, nor does enforcement of the statute require invasions of the conjugal bedroom."

Despite the district court's ruling that Jane Roe had legal standing, the state of Texas continued its argument that *Roe v. Wade* was moot, or legally invalid. The state argued that Jane Roe had long since given birth and therefore no longer had any opportunity to benefit from an overturning of the abortion law.

Doe v. Bolton

The Court had also agreed to hear another abortion case, this one from Georgia. *Doe v. Bolton* pitted a twenty-two-year-old mother of three, pregnant again by her husband who then deserted the family, against Georgia's more liberal, though still highly restrictive, abortion law. Unlike the one-hundred-year-old Texas law, the Georgia law had just been passed in an effort to moderate abortion restrictions. Despite this liberalization, it still only permitted abortions determined to be "medically therapeutic." It allowed a "physician duly licensed" in Georgia to perform abortions in situations where continuing a pregnancy potentially jeopardized the woman's life or posed a threat of serious or permanent injury. The Georgia law also allowed abortion when there was a strong likelihood that the child would be born with "a grave, permanent, and irremediable mental or physical defect," and in cases of rape.

Mary Doe did not meet the standards set by this law. She, like Jane Roe, simply did not want to bring another child into the world. The three-judge panel in the federal district court in Atlanta ruled similarly to their counterparts in Dallas—they found the Georgia law unconstitutional though failed to issue injunctive relief (an order instructing the state of Georgia to stop prosecuting violators of the law).

Doe v. Bolton raised a much broader range of issues than did *Roe v. Wade*. The Texas law denied abortion under any circumstances. The Georgia law defined very specific circumstances under which a woman could obtain an abortion. It required a

WHO'S ON FIRST?

When New York lawyer Roy Lucas first offered his help and expertise, *Roe* attorneys Sarah Weddington and Linda Coffee were both appreciative and excited. Lucas brought a level of knowledge about constitutional matters and Supreme Court procedures that neither woman had. They felt his involvement would give their case a much-needed boost. But as the big date loomed near, it became increasingly clear that Lucas had a different view of his role.

In the beginning, it was easy to let Lucas take the lead. He was the expert, after all, and he had the time both Weddington and Coffee lacked. Preliminary documents listing him as the lead attorney raised eyebrows but didn't draw any further attention until Weddington realized that Court rules typically allotted one attorney thirty minutes to present the oral arguments for each side. Lucas planned to be that attorney, and as preparations progressed, he began treating Weddington and Coffee more like underlings than colleagues. Once she saw what was happening, Weddington hurriedly petitioned the Court for permission for both her and Lucas to present arguments.

A photo of Linda Coffee on the ten-year anniversary of the Roe v. Wade *decision.*

Coffee pointed out that having two attorneys share arguments was highly unusual, an arrangement the Court was likely to allow only if each attorney offered something unique. Lucas had nothing unique to contribute to the case beyond his understanding of constitutional law and judicial process, and putting him in the role of colead would look like what it was—a power struggle. This would make the *Roe* team appear amateurish and ill prepared. Coffee stepped in and simply sent a letter to the Court stating that Weddington would be the lead attorney who would address the Court; she sent copies to Lucas and the Texas attorneys as well. Though privately furious, Lucas publicly behaved as though that had been his intent all along. Coffee's quick action turned what could have been a disastrous divisiveness into a professionalism that allowed the appeal to proceed smoothly.

woman who wanted an abortion to undergo independent examinations by three physicians. All three had to agree that an abortion was justified. The physicians then had to put their opinions regarding the need for an abortion in writing. The law mandated that only hospitals certified by the Joint Commission on Accreditation of Hospitals could perform abortions, and each abortion had to be approved in advance by the hospital's abortion committee. The Georgia law included additional record-keeping requirements as well.

These requirements, argued *Doe*, put the state in the position of not only interfering with a medical decision that rightfully rested with a woman and her physician but actually dictating the procedures for making such decisions. No other laws attempted to manage medical decisions for other conditions in this way; there was no law, for example, that required a patient with heart disease to obtain concurring opinions from three different physicians before undergoing heart surgery. The restrictive Georgia law infringed on a woman's right to privacy as well as on a physician's ability to make medical decisions. The U.S. District Court for the Northern District of Georgia in Atlanta ruled that significant portions of the Georgia law were unconstitutional, and the Supreme Court agreed to hear the appeal.

Changes in the Court

In September, just two weeks before the scheduled start of the Supreme Court's 1971 session, Justices Hugo Black and John Harlan resigned for health reasons. Justice Black, who had written the Court's majority opinion in *United States v. Vuitch*, died a week later. The two vacancies meant two new appointments— from Richard Nixon, a conservative president whose anti-abortion views were well known. The turn of events postponed the Court's session.

As expected, President Nixon's nominations reflected his conservative leanings. Lewis Powell was a practicing attorney from Virginia, and former president of the American Bar Association. William Rehnquist had clerked for Justice Robert Jackson during the *Brown v. Board of Education* desegregation case in the

William Rehnquist (left) and Lewis Powell after being sworn in to the Supreme Court in 1971. The new justices would not take the bench until after the first arguments for Roe v. Wade *were heard.*

1950s and was widely known as a political conservative. The *Roe* attorneys expected the Court's changes to delay their appeals until the two new justices took the bench after January 1, but the Court surprised them by rescheduling the cases for December 13. This meant the new justices would not participate.

This was a relief to the *Roe* and *Doe* teams, who were not eager to see two more conservatives join the then-moderate Court. Texas assistant attorney general Jay Floyd was not pleased, however. He wanted the full Court, with its new conservative members, to hear the appeal. He filed a motion requesting that the appeal be delayed until the two vacancies were filled. The Court unanimously denied the motion. Both sides entered their final preparations for their appearance before a seven-member Court.

Chapter 4

May It Please the Court

DECEMBER 13, 1971, DAWNED as a pleasant winter day in
Washington, D.C. Demonstrators milled quietly outside
the front doors of the Supreme Court building when the attorneys began arriving. Beyond the ornate, heavy doors was a world
of form and protocol, from the instruction notes handed to arriving attorneys to the seating arrangements in the courtroom.

The courtroom was very formal, with tall marble columns
and a high ceiling. Heavy velvet curtains shrouded the room's
entrances, one in the back where spectators and attorneys
entered and one in the front behind the justices' bench. Pewlike
sections offered seating for those fortunate enough to have
reserved them or to have special Supreme Court press passes.
Others who were interested in seeing the Court in action could
do so for precisely three minutes at a time, ushered in a contin-
ual rotation of small groups to sit in a special tourist section. The
justices sat at the front of the room, arranged according to senior-
ity on the Court, with the chief justice seated in the center.
Attorneys presenting oral arguments addressed the justices from
a small podium directly in front of the chief justice.

Court proceedings were punctual and precise. A large clock
hanging on the wall directly behind the chief justice's seat
served as a constant reminder that each attorney had exactly
thirty minutes to speak. Small lights on the podium reinforced
the time limitations, with white signaling time was almost up
and red sending the unmistakable message that it had expired.
Roe v. Wade arguments were scheduled to begin at 10:00 A.M., followed by *Doe v. Bolton* an hour later.

The Court's marshal opened the day's hearings by calling the Court to order with the salutation that had been an element of Court ritual since 1789.

> The honorable, the chief justice and the associate justices of the Supreme Court of the United States. Oyez, oyez, oyez, all persons having business before the honorable, the Supreme Court of the United States, are admonished to draw near and give their attention, for the Court is now sitting. God save the United States and this honorable court.

The United States Supreme Court building, where Roe v. Wade *arguments opened on December 13, 1971.*

As those in the courtroom stood, the velvet curtains behind the bench parted. The justices entered the courtroom single file and took their places. From right to left facing the audience, the seven who would rule on the two abortion cases were Harry Blackmun, Byron White, William Brennan Jr., Warren Burger, William Douglas, Potter Stewart, and Thurgood Marshall. When all the justices were present, they took their seats. Clerks passed out the briefs and other papers the justices would use to guide the hearings, and at 10:07 A.M. Chief Justice Burger invited Sarah Weddington to begin.

Weddington Presents Her Case

It has often been said that good oral arguments seldom win a case, but bad oral arguments can easily lose one. The justices are very well prepared when the hearings begin, having had several weeks to read the submitted briefs and relevant comments prepared by their clerks. Typically the justices have specific questions or clarifications in mind that they address to the attorneys. Weddington had carefully prepared and practiced a presentation. She planned to use her thirty minutes in two segments, twenty-five minutes initially and five minutes reserved for rebuttal, as court procedure allowed. Knowing the justices could, and would likely, interrupt, she also had a short list of key points she knew she had to make.

The first question came within minutes, when Chief Justice Burger wanted to know if the Court's recent ruling in *United States v. Vuitch* hadn't in fact already decided several key issues in *Roe v. Wade*. Weddington explained her belief that it had not, pointing out that *Vuitch* had focused on the vagueness of the word *health*. While the Texas law's vagueness was certainly a factor, the primary issues in *Roe* centered on violations of various constitutional guarantees.

Weddington continued her presentation with a discussion of what she felt were key points of the case, the effect of a pregnancy on a woman's life and a woman's right to choose whether to continue that pregnancy. She told the justices,

A pregnancy to a woman is perhaps one of the most determinative aspects of her life. It disrupts her body, it disrupts her entire family life. Because of the impact on the woman, this certainly, in as far as there are any rights which are fundamental, is a matter which is of such fundamental and basic concern to the woman involved that she should be allowed to make the choice as to whether to continue or to terminate her pregnancy.

Justice Stewart interrupted to commend Weddington for the points she had made so far, then asked when she was going to get to the constitutional issues that she had said were underlying the abortion issue. Weddington responded by citing the Ninth Amendment's protection of unenumerated rights. In doing so, she referenced a recent article by respected constitutional scholar Cyril Means. In the article, Means pointed out that at the

Justice Potter Stewart questioned plaintiff's attorney Sarah Weddington about the constitutionality of the Texas abortion law.

Sarah Weddington cited the Ninth and Fourteenth Amendments to the Constitution to support her position in Roe v. Wade.

time of the Ninth Amendment's ratification in 1791, there were no laws that prohibited abortion. Until the first of such laws was passed some thirty years later, abortions were legally available to any women who sought them. At the time the Ninth Amendment was drafted, the right to choose an abortion rested with the individual woman. It was reasonable to conclude, Means wrote, that the amendment's authors intended for the Ninth Amendment to include all rights commonly held at the time of its writing as "unenumerated."

Weddington also delicately referenced the Court's divided opinion in *Griswold v. Connecticut*, noting that the justices themselves seemed uncertain "as to the specific constitutional framework of the right which they held to exist." While the Court in that decision had upheld Griswold's right to distribute birth control information and devices, the various opinions from the justices cited a range of amendments as the foundations for the rights they were upholding. The entire matter of a personal right to privacy, Weddington implied, did in fact exist in numerous constitutional contexts. This should serve to strengthen, not dilute, its constitutional protection.

Everything but the Kitchen Sink

Justice Stewart then asked if *Roe*'s position relied on the Fourteenth Amendment's due process clause. Weddington replied that it did, then, in an effort to drive home her earlier point, she quickly added that it relied on the Fourteenth Amendment's equal protection clause as well, and on the Ninth Amendment and "a variety of others." Seeing humor in the unintended "everything but the kitchen sink" image Weddington's response evoked, Justice Stewart drew a laugh from the audience by interjecting, "and anything else that might obtain."

Weddington laughed, too, then returned to her point that the Constitution broadly and variously protected individual rights. She told the Court,

> I think that in as far as the Court has said that there is a penumbra that exists to encompass the entire purpose of the Constitution, that I think one of the purposes of the Constitution was to guarantee to the individual the right to determine the course of their own lives.

Questions from the justices continued. Knowing the state of Texas would argue that the fetus was an individual in its own regard, Justices Stewart and White pressed Weddington on the issue of whether the state rightfully had an interest in protecting the fetus during at least some stages of pregnancy. When, the justices wanted to know, did a fetus have protections as a person under the Constitution? Acknowledging that there were notable emotional issues in late-term abortion, Weddington replied that the state might rightfully have an interest in protecting a fetus that could survive on its own.

However, she noted, neither the states nor the Constitution treated a fetus as an individual person with full rights until it was born. This was most clearly stated in the Fourteenth Amendment, which assigned citizenship to "all persons born . . . in the United States." Weddington returned to the article by Cyril Means to make her final point on the issue.

> The Constitution, as I read it, and as interpreted and documented by Professor Means, attaches protection to the person at the time of birth. Those persons born are citizens. Under the enumeration clause, we count those people who are born.

The justices asked other questions about the appropriateness of including Dr. Hallford as a plaintiff. Though the plaintiffs were all connected because the same abortion law affected them, Dr. Hallford's standing was a different issue. His involvement in the case argued that the Texas law failed to provide clear guidance about when he, as a physician, could legally perform an abortion. While the right to privacy was not an issue for Dr. Hallford as it was for Roe and Doe, the physician faced criminal charges for having performed abortions that law enforcement officials determined were in violation of the law. Weddington noted that whether or not the physician's inclusion was appropriate, the legal standing of the women who were the other plaintiffs in the case remained unaffected. They still suffered irreparable injury as a result of the Texas law's infringement upon their right to privacy.

After a few more minutes of discussion about fetal rights, the Court clerk signaled Weddington that she had five of her allotted minutes left. Though frustrated that she hadn't made it through the presentation she had so carefully prepared, Weddington wanted to save those five minutes for rebuttal comments following arguments from the state of Texas, so she took her seat. Though she had not covered all of the key points she wanted to make, she managed to cover those that were essential despite digressive questioning from the justices. Most important, she retained her composure under pressure, shaped her responses to return focus to constitutional issues, and made no major mistakes.

Off on the Wrong Foot

Jay Floyd, representing the state of Texas, was not so fortunate. His opening comment met with complete silence from the audience and from the bench. "It's an old joke, but when a man argues against two beautiful ladies like this, they're going to have the last word."

Though the justices often used humor to lighten the tension that typically filled the courtroom, and had done so throughout Weddington's arguments, they did so in what they felt was a pro-

WHEN DOES LIFE BEGIN?

Religious and philosophical beliefs about when life begins are nearly as diverse as the individuals who hold them. Many faiths, such as the Roman Catholic religion, believe that conception represents a divine act and marks the beginning of human life. Other belief systems accept birth as the point of physical and spiritual life.

From a social perspective, birth is a triumphant event marked by much celebration at its occurrence and annually throughout life. All records of human existence begin with birth; in most cultures, the birth certificate represents official proof of that existence.

Technology continues to push belief systems and scientific boundaries, presenting ethicists and legal experts alike with new dilemmas. Scientists can fertilize an egg in the laboratory, cultivate the resulting zygote into an embryo, and deep-freeze it. When retrieved and thawed, the embryo can be implanted into a woman's uterus and develop as normally as if the process had occurred naturally. Advances in medical technology have also made it possible for physicians to save infants born at gestational ages as early as twenty-six weeks, raising new ethical issues about late-term abortions and fetal viability.

---

fessional manner. Floyd's attempted joke undercut this professionalism by casting the perception that Floyd did not take his female opponents, and by extension their case and the Court, seriously. The joke was particularly inappropriate given the nature of *Roe* and its arguments of constitutional protection for a right specific to women. It also did not sit well in a social climate that was becoming known as the dawn of the women's rights era.

The silence surprised and unnerved Floyd, who didn't seem to understand the magnitude of his gaffe. After a moment's pause, he moved directly into the beginning of his arguments, and another blunder. Repeating the mistake he made in the first trial, Floyd asserted that the case was moot because Jane Roe was no longer pregnant and therefore had no legal standing to bring suit. Justice Stewart swiftly challenged the assertion, noting that *Roe* was a class action. Since "there are at any given time unmarried pregnant females in the state of Texas," Justice Stewart observed, Jane Roe's personal condition had no bearing on the case's legal standing.

Inexplicably, Floyd pursued the mootness issue until Justice Stewart again interrupted to ask him what he thought would constitute legal standing for a woman who wanted to challenge the state's restrictions on abortion. "What procedure would you suggest for any pregnant female in the state of Texas ever to get any judicial consideration of this constitutional claim?" Stewart queried.

There was no such procedure, Floyd answered, adding that a woman made her choice prior to becoming pregnant and after that "no remedy is provided." The response provoked a biting retort from Justice Stewart that perhaps the real moment of choice occurred when a woman decided to live in Texas. The courtroom erupted in laughter. Somewhat miffed, Floyd asked if he could proceed. When Justice Stewart nodded, Floyd attempted a weak comeback by saying, "There's no restriction on moving, you know."

What Floyd didn't realize, legal analysts later noted, was that he had once again insulted the Court. Though Floyd did not intend for his response to sound flippant, the Court took it as a continuation of the brand of humor with which he had tried to start his presentation. Justice Stewart's quip and the laughter it evoked belied the bench's disapproval with what appeared to them to be Floyd's belittling of women.

Unanswerable Questions

Decorum returned with more questions from the justices. Why did the state not punish women who attempted or obtained abortions? To Floyd's response that perhaps Texas should consider murder charges, the justices pointed out that even the Texas statute did not equate abortion with murder. Further questioning forced Floyd to concede that the state also did not consistently enforce its law. Floyd became more hesitant as the justices pushed him for scientific evidence to support the state's position that life began at the "moment of impregnation." He directed the justices to the state's brief, which outlined the development of the human embryo into a fetus "from about seven to nine days after conception."

What about six days? Justice Marshall wanted to know. Or five days, or four? "This statute goes all the way back to one hour," he noted.

Floyd's frustration was clear as he fumbled to respond. There were "unanswerable questions in this field," he finally offered, a comment that brought laughter from the courtroom once again. Realizing that the words he spoke were not at all the ones he intended, Floyd acknowledged that the entire line of response was "an artless statement on our part." Attempting to allow Floyd a chance to recover his composure, Justice Marshall said he withdrew his question. Unfortunately Floyd was not able to stop with a simple thank you. "That's really when the soul comes into the unborn, if a person believes in a soul, I don't know," he added, confusing everyone, including, apparently, himself.

In the final minutes of the state's arguments, Floyd fumbled several references to previous Court rulings and generally faltered in his presentation. While acknowledging that the plaintiffs were relying on the Ninth Amendment to support their assertions, Floyd made no effort to offer an argument as to why they shouldn't. His rambling response that there would be no

Justice Thurgood Marshall (pictured) stumped defense attorney Jay Floyd by questioning Texas's determination of the moment when life begins.

grounds for a privacy ruling if the *Doe* plaintiffs were removed from *Roe v. Wade* as Texas hoped they would be seemed more like wishing aloud, and again Floyd appeared to confuse both himself and the Court. His inability to refute the arguments Weddington and Coffee put forth made it embarrassingly evident that Floyd never expected the Court to accept *Roe*'s constitutional protection arguments as valid.

The justices took a last stab at the issue of choice with Justice Stewart noting that the Texas law made no accommodations for women who became pregnant after being raped. Such women had no choice in the matter, he pointed out in a clear reference to Floyd's earlier comments that a woman's choice about pregnancy ended when she became pregnant. Floyd's time ran out while he struggled to formulate a response. Weddington returned to the podium for five minutes of rebuttal, which she used to reiterate key points about the Ninth Amendment and the right to privacy.

Slightly more than an hour after it started, the Supreme Court hearing of *Roe v. Wade* was over.

Chapter 5

Back to Square One: The Court Requests Rearguments

NOW THERE WAS NOTHING to do except wait for the Court's decision, expected sometime in early 1972. Most of the *Roe v. Wade* players returned to jobs and lives put on hold while preparing for their appearance before the Supreme Court. All were soon busy, and pushed *Roe* to the backs of their minds.

Only Sarah Weddington was left to start anew in both career and life. She had given up her job as an assistant city attorney to accept a temporary position at Roy Lucas's James Madison Constitutional Law Institute while preparing for the *Roe* trial. Now that the trial was over, that job was gone. So too was her marriage, though she had been too wrapped up in *Roe* to notice. Looking for both a change of pace and a way to help shape a more favorable political environment for women, Weddington set out to win a seat in the Texas House of Representatives.

Meanwhile, behind the closed doors of the Supreme Court's inner chambers, a tempest brewed. Though the issues of abortion and a woman's right to privacy were complex and not entirely clear-cut from a legal perspective, the justices appeared inclined to uphold the district court's finding at the end of their first meeting. Instead, politically motivated delays and infighting among the justices postponed the decision and ultimately resulted in the Court making a rare request to rehear the *Roe* arguments. What could have been a relatively rapid and straightforward decision had the Court written its opinion promptly was instead churning toward an explosive divisiveness that would threaten the very structure of the Court before finally being resolved.

Behind Closed Doors

As was their practice, the justices met to discuss *Roe v. Wade* a few days after hearing its oral arguments. It was in this setting that decisions and dissensions took shape, as the justices reviewed relevant briefs and their notes taken during the attorneys' presentations. Often, they left these meetings knowing what the Court's majority opinion would be and who would write it.

Chief Justice Burger led the discussion by summarizing what he perceived as the key points. He believed that if the Texas law was unconstitutional as the district court held, Jane Roe did have legal standing, and the class represented in the suit (all women in

After hearing the arguments Chief Justice Warren Burger privately expressed his opinion that the Texas law was archaic, but not unconstitutional.

Texas who were or could become pregnant) were entitled to the injunction the suit sought. The primary issue in such circumstances, he said, was how to balance "the state's interest in protecting fetal life and a woman's interest in not having children." However, he ended his comments by concluding that, while the Texas law was "certainly archaic and obsolete," he could not find it either vague or unconstitutional. The chief justice's view left little room for misunderstanding. Just because a law was bad, as he believed this one was, it wasn't necessarily unconstitutional.

Justice Douglas vehemently disagreed. The Texas law was unquestionably unconstitutional, he insisted, in its violation of a woman's right to privacy. It was also unconstitutionally vague in that it failed to provide appropriate guidance for physicians to know where they stood legally when making a decision concerning whether an abortion was necessary to save a woman's life, the only situation under which the Texas law permitted abortion.

Taking Sides

Justices Brennan and Stewart sided with Justice Douglas, though Justice Stewart raised the concept of the state's right to establish certain requirements, including that abortions be performed only by licensed physicians. This was a reasonable restriction, he felt, as well as being consistent with other statutory requirements regulating medical care. Knowing they would discuss this issue in great detail in their deliberations on *Doe v. Bolton*, which challenged the extensive restrictions Georgia law placed on medical practitioners as well as procedures, the justices did not take the discussion any further within the context of *Roe*.

They did discuss another restriction, the state's ability to legislate that a woman could not obtain an abortion "after a certain period of pregnancy." Justice Stewart pushed discussion on this point, which would later become crucial in the Court's majority opinion. Justice Marshall joined in this concern, presenting his position that if an aborted fetus "came out breathing . . . to kill it is murder."

Justice White saw the situation a bit differently than did his colleagues. The real issue, he said, was that women wanted the right to end a pregnancy simply because it was unwanted, without regard for health reasons. Within this framework, the real question was "Does the state have police power to protect a fetus that has life in it as opposed to the desire of the mother?" Justice White believed the state did have such power as delegated by the Tenth Amendment, which granted to the states all powers not delegated to or prohibited by the federal government. The Texas law operated within this power, he felt, and therefore did not violate the Constitution.

Justice Blackmun agreed with various points broached by the other justices and disagreed with others. He challenged Justice Marshall's assertion that the Fourteenth Amendment would cover the constitutional issues *Roe* raised, saying that although Jane Roe did have Fourteenth Amendment rights, the amendment gave "no absolute right to do with one's body what you like" and therefore did not apply in this case. The Ninth Amendment did apply, however, and the Texas law infringed upon it, Justice Blackmun said. He would affirm the Dallas court's judgment, and also "go so far as to grant an injunction" to keep the state from enforcing the law.

By the end of the meeting, it appeared the justices were to make a 5-2 decision to affirm the lower court's ruling in *Roe v. Wade* that the Texas law was unconstitutional (though the notes made by some justices reflected a 6-1 division). Such a decision would effectively nullify the law, granting the *Roe* team's desire for the injunction that Justice Blackmun also favored. The matter was not to be resolved so smoothly, however. Incomplete notes, differing recollections, and judicial politics ultimately pushed the case into a reargument.

Disagreements Boil Over

The U.S. Supreme Court is steeped in tradition, from the invocation that opens every Court session to the order in which the justices speak in their deliberations (most senior to least senior). Similarly, the chief justice assigns the writing of the Court's decisions when he is among the majority. When he is not, the task of making such assignment falls to the most senior justice who is.

Though Chief Justice Burger was a dissenting opinion in both *Roe v. Wade* and *Doe v. Bolton,* he nonetheless assigned the cases to Justice Blackmun. This angered Justice Douglas, who felt that as the most senior justice among the majority, he should have made the assignments. While he didn't disagree with the selection of Justice Blackmun to write the *Roe* decision, Justice Douglas viewed the breach of protocol as an intentional slight.

Justice Douglas fired off a polite but pointed memo to Chief Justice Burger suggesting that one of the four justices who was in the majority on *Doe* instead write that decision. The attempt by Justice Douglas to reassert his authority instead spurred a response that was the first hint of looming trouble. His own recollection of the discussion was that it had not yielded a firm tally in either case, Chief Justice Burger noted, writing to Justice Douglas,

Justice Harry Blackmun was appointed to write the Court's opinions for Roe v. Wade *and* Doe v. Bolton.

> I therefore marked down no votes and said this was a case that would have to stand or fall on the writing, when it was done. That is still my view of how to handle these two sensitive cases, which, I might add, are quite probable candidates for reargument [after Justices Powell and Rehnquist join the Court].

Still fuming over the chief justice's impropriety in assigning the opinions, Justice Douglas missed the significance of the suggestion to reargue. By his recollection there had been a clear and definitive majority, so there would be no reason to hear the case again. It was an oversight that would further divide the two justices.

The issue arose again shortly after the start of the new year. Justices Powell and Rehnquist brought the Court back to its full complement of nine, and Chief Justice Burger asked for recommendations about which cases should be reargued before the full Court. Justice Blackmun was no happier about being assigned to write the *Roe* and *Doe* opinions than was Justice Douglas about being usurped in making the assignments. Seeing an opportunity to resolve his discomfort and the squabble between Justice Douglas and Chief Justice Burger, Justice Blackmun suggested the two abortion cases be reargued. The Court took no further action on the suggestion, however, and Justice Blackmun reluctantly wrote his first draft on *Roe*.

The First Draft Evokes an Angry Response

Much to the surprise of his colleagues, and to the anger of those in the majority, the draft was short (just seventeen pages) and evaded the constitutional issues the case sought to resolve, namely the right to privacy and vagueness. The issue of unconstitutional vagueness was sufficient to affirm the case on its merits, Justice Blackmun wrote in the cover memo to the draft. Even though this had been a secondary argument, Justice Blackmun wanted to assign it primary status in the opinion. Doing so, he noted, would make it unnecessary to address the "more complex Ninth Amendment issue."

A furious Justice Brennan fired a response back summarizing his differing recollection of the December 16 meeting. He requested that the opinion be revised precisely to address that more complex issue. The Ninth Amendment was by far the more significant issue brought forth by *Roe*, Justice Brennan believed, and it was essential for the Court to deal with its issues up front and directly. He felt the Court's majority shared this belief, and urged Justice Blackmun to address it as such.

> In the circumstances, I would prefer a disposition of the core constitutional question. Your circulation, however, invalidates the Texas statute only on the vagueness

ground. . . . I think we should dispose of both cases on the ground supported by the majority. This does not mean, however, that I disagree with your conclusion as to the vagueness of the Texas statute. I only feel that there is no point in delaying any longer our confrontation with the core issue on which there appears to be a majority and which would make reaching the vagueness issue unnecessary.

The response that Justice Douglas, who had been working on his own version of a draft decision, sent to Justice Blackmun the following day was even more curt. Though he again dredged up his discontent over the way the assignment to write the opinion had been made, Justice Douglas also confronted Justice Blackmun's recollection of the deliberations.

My notes confirm what Bill Brennan wrote yesterday in his memo to you—that abortion statutes were invalid save as they required that an abortion be performed by a licensed physician within a limited time after conception. That was the clear view of a majority of the seven who heard the argument. My notes also indicate that the Chief had the opposed view, which made it puzzling as to why he made the assignment at all except that he indicated he might affirm on vagueness. . . . So I think we should meet what Bill Brennan calls the "core issue."

Justice William Brennan found the Texas abortion law unconstitutional.

Justice Douglas also made clear that he, like Justice Brennan, saw no reason to reargue the *Doe v. Bolton* case. An exchange of memos

DR. HALLFORD AND THE TEXAS DOES

Two other plaintiffs joined their cases to *Roe v. Wade*, physician James Hallford and a married couple identified as the Does. The Court's opinion addressed their issues as well.

The Court upheld Dr. Hallford's legal standing, or right to bring his issues to court. Because the rest of the opinion invalidated the Texas law prohibiting abortion, and because the Court issued an injunction to prevent the state from prosecuting those charged with violating the law, Texas was required to drop the criminal charges pending against Dr. Hallford.

While acknowledging that the Does had issues similar to *Roe*, the Court ruled that their case lacked standing because Mrs. Doe was not pregnant. Rather, she objected to the Texas law on the basis of a series of events and consequences that might happen were she to become pregnant. The Supreme Court found the speculative nature of this position inadequate "to present an actual case or controversy."

---

and drafts continued over the next few weeks. Finally Justice Blackmun issued a memo formally recommending both cases be reargued, citing concerns about the emotional and sensitive nature of abortion and his uncertainty about the details of the cases. Justice Douglas shot back a response within an hour setting out his strong belief that the Court should "get the cases down," or finished, without rearguments. The majority, he noted, would still be a majority in a nine-member Court. None seemed ambivalent in their positions.

> I have a feeling that where the Court is split 4-4 or 4-2-1 or even in an important constitutional case 4-3, reargument may be desirable. But you have a firm 5 and the firm 5 will be behind you in these two opinions until they come down. It is a difficult field and a difficult subject. But where there is that solid agreement of the majority I think it is important to announce the cases, and let the result be known so that the legislature can go to work and draft their new laws.

Chief Justice Burger's response affirmed Justice Douglas's suspicions that a political agenda was at work. His memo openly stated his desire to change the balance of the Court's vote by adding its newest members to the mix.

I have had a great many problems with these cases from the outset. They are not as simple for me as they appear to be for others. The States have, I think, as much concern in this area as in any within their province; federal power has only that which can be traced to a specific provision of the Constitution. . . . I vote to reargue early in the next Term.

Seeing an opportunity to possibly sway the vote to change the majority opinion, dissenting justices Powell and Rehnquist also voiced their support for reargument. When it became clear that Chief Justice Burger had enough votes on the Court to force the matter and intended to use them, Justice Douglas's anger exploded. In a terse note to the chief justice, Justice Douglas threatened to publicly expose the Court's internal dispute: "If the vote of the Conference is to reargue, then I will file a statement telling what is happening to us and the tragedy it entails."

"A Destructive Force"

Before leaving for summer vacation, Justice Douglas took the first steps to make good on his threat. In a scathing memo he blasted the chief justice's behavior, writing,

There is a destructive force at work in the Court. When a Chief Justice tries to bend the Court to his will by manipulating assignments, the integrity of the institution is imperiled. The votes are firm. The cases should therefore be announced. The plea that the cases be reargued is merely strategy by a minority somehow to suppress the majority view with the hope that exigencies of time will change the result. . . . That kind of strategy dilutes the integrity of the Court and makes the decisions here depend on the manipulative skill of a Chief Justice.

Justice Douglas retreated to his summer home in Washington State. Through an exchange of letters with Justice Brennan, Justice Douglas finally cooled down and agreed that it would be a mistake to publicly air the Court's internal disagreements, so he withdrew his memo. On June 26, 1972, the Court announced its decision to reargue sixteen cases altogether; the abortion cases *Roe v. Wade* and *Doe v. Bolton* were among them.

Just a week after the Court's announcement, Justice Douglas's angry memo was the focus of a front-page story in the *Washington Post*. After all Justice Brennan's work to calm his colleague into retracting the memo, someone leaked it to the press. Never before had the inner workings of the U.S. Supreme Court been so public, and the impression this glimpse offered of the country's top jurists was unflattering to say the least. A horrified Justice Douglas quickly wrote to Chief Justice Burger and the justices.

> I am upset and appalled. I have never breathed a word concerning these cases, or my memo, to anyone outside the Court. I have no idea where the writer got the story. We have our differences; but so far as I am concerned they are wholly internal; and if revealed, they are mirrored in opinions filed, never in "leaks" to the press.

In an angry memo, Justice William Douglas described the actions of the chief justice as manipulative. That memo, later retracted by Douglas, was leaked to the press.

The justices had already left for summer vacation, however, and by the time they returned in the fall the dispute was old history.

Revisiting Familiar Ground

The decision to reargue *Roe v. Wade* and *Doe v. Bolton* caught both sides by surprise. The Court sent notification on September 5, 1972, that the rearguments would take place on October 11.

Sarah Weddington interrupted her campaign for Texas state representative to prepare a supplemental brief citing court cases that had taken place since the original arguments had been heard nearly a year earlier. She also called on *Roe* supporters in the legal community to set up moot, or practice, court sessions to help her refine her presentation.

The state of Texas replaced Jay Floyd with his boss Robert Flowers, the chief of the Texas Attorney General's Enforcement Division. At first the move appeared to indicate that the state was taking the reargument hearing more seriously than it had taken the original appeal. However, Flowers prepared no additional materials for the Court to review. In posttrial interviews, he acknowledged that he did not even prepare an outline for his appearance before the Court.

Representing the plaintiff, Weddington was again first to address the Court. After summarizing the case's history, she confidently led the justices through her key points. This time there were few questions from the Court. The only significant challenge came when Justice Blackmun pursued the relationship between *Roe* and the Court's recent ruling that the death penalty violated the Eighth Amendment's prohibition of cruel and unusual punishment. If the fetus could be considered a person at any stage of development before birth, the Court could be perceived as inconsistent if it said that ending a fetus's life through abortion was not cruel and unusual punishment. Weddington reiterated a key point from earlier presentations: The Constitution did not consider the fetus a person.

This response opened the door for Justice Stewart and Chief Justice Burger to question the constitutionality of the state to establish the fetus as a person. Weddington deflected the matter

DOE V. BOLTON

Though equally important in its effect on abortion laws throughout the country, *Doe v. Bolton* concerned more narrowly defined issues and practices. It has been largely overshadowed by the obvious and far-reaching implications of *Roe v. Wade*.

The Court upheld the lower court's decision striking the law's accredited hospital, multiple-physician certification, and hospital committee approval requirements. The Court left intact, however, the state's authority to impose restrictions on abortion.

Legal analysts expect *Doe v. Bolton* to take on increasing significance as states look for ways to balance the constitutional rights and issues decided in *Roe* with their interests in regulating abortion.

by responding that only the Supreme Court could determine the meaning of the federal Constitution, not the states. His interest piqued, Justice White pushed the issue further. "If it were established that an unborn fetus is a person, you would have almost an impossible case here, would you not?"

The hypothesis, or imagined scenario, forced Weddington to concede that she would then "have a very difficult case."

Robert Flowers began his presentation on behalf of the state of Texas with an equally familiar premise, arguing that the state held that "upon conception we had a human being, a person within the concept of the Constitution." It took less than ten minutes for Flowers's lack of preparation to catch up with him. Like Jay Floyd before him, Flowers faltered when Justice Stewart asked for evidence of any case that supported this premise. Questioning from Justice Blackmun forced the additional concession that "the medical profession itself is not in agreement as to when life begins." Justice White revisited the issue of establishing the fetus as a person, saying "You've lost your case, then, if the fetus or the embryo is not a person, is that it?" Robert Flowers was forced again to concede.

When the rearguments ended, no one in the courtroom felt comfortable speculating about the outcome. There were just no clear signs which way the Court was leaning, and once again it was time to wait.

A Watershed Decision

The Court seemed to set aside the hostility and ego battles that marred its first round with *Roe*. Justice Blackmun had done considerable research into the medical aspects of abortion, which he incorporated into the draft decision he circulated just six weeks after the reargument. In this draft, Justice Blackmun identified a distinct separation between the first and subsequent trimesters of pregnancy. The separation gave a woman the right to choose abortion without state-imposed restrictions before the end of the first trimester, and it gave states the right to evaluate and regulate abortions after that point in the pregnancy.

Though there was some discussion about whether viability or gestational term was the better measure for limiting abortions, the draft received strong support from the majority. Justice Blackmun actively solicited comments from his colleagues,

Upon being questioned about the defense's view that life begins at conception, Robert Flowers admitted that there was no medical evidence to support this conclusion.

which he then incorporated into subsequent drafts. By mid-January he achieved a final draft, and the Court set January 22, 1973, as the date it would announce its decision to uphold the Texas district court's findings. Chief Justice Burger joined Justices Blackmun, Douglas, Brennan, Stewart, Marshall, and Powell in the decision. Justices White and Rehnquist dissented.

The Supreme Court presented its decision to a packed courtroom at precisely 10:00 A.M. Justice Blackmun read an eight-page summary of the fifty-one-page majority opinion. He started with what was for the Court a rare acknowledgment of the emotional overtones that characterized the abortion issue.

> We forthwith acknowledge our awareness of the sensitive and emotional nature of the abortion controversy, of the vigorous opposing views, even among physicians, and of the deep and seemingly absolute convictions that the subject inspires. One's philosophy, one's experiences, one's exposure to the raw edges of human existence, one's religious training, one's attitudes toward life and family and their values, and the moral standards one establishes and seeks to observe, are all likely to influence and to color one's thinking and conclusions about abortion.

> In addition, population growth, pollution, poverty, and racial overtones tend to complicate and not to simplify the problem.

> Our task, of course, is to resolve the issue by constitutional measurement, free of emotion and of predilection. We seek earnestly to do this, and because we do, we have inquired into, and in this opinion place some emphasis upon, medical and medical-legal history and what that history reveals about man's attitudes toward the abortion procedure over the centuries.

The majority opinion cited the key points of the case, upholding the district court's ruling in each. It also did what the district court decision failed to do—it granted injunctive relief to

Dissenting Opinions

Justices White and Rehnquist disagreed with the Court's majority opinion, and they issued dissenting opinions to explain why. They read their dissents during the Court's public presentation of its opinion.

Justice White's dissent criticized his colleagues directly, a rather unusual action. He began by accusing the justices who voted with the majority of holding that "the Constitution of the United States values the convenience, whim or caprice of the putative mother more than the life or potential life of the fetus." His harsh comments were brief but forceful.

> I find nothing in the language or history of the Constitution to support the Court's judgment. The Court simply fashions and announces a new constitutional right for pregnant mothers. . . .
> As an exercise of raw judicial power, the Court perhaps has authority to do what it does today; but in my view its judgment is an improvident and extravagant exercise of the power of judicial review.

Justice Rehnquist focused his comments on the issues presented by the cases. In particular he attacked the Court's liberal, and in his view incorrect, interpretation of the Fourteenth Amendment.

> The Due Process Clause of the Fourteenth Amendment undoubtedly does place a limit, albeit a broad one, on legislative power to enact laws such as this. . . . But the Court's sweeping invalidation of any restrictions on abortion during the first trimester is impossible to justify under that standard, and the conscious weighing of competing factors that the Court's opinion apparently substitutes for the established test is far more appropriate to a legislative judgment than to a judicial one. . . . The decision here to break pregnancy into three distinct terms and to outline the permissible restrictions the State may impose in each one, for example, partakes more of judicial legislation than it does of a determination of the intent of the drafters of the Fourteenth Amendment.

prevent the state of Texas from continuing to enforce its law prohibiting abortion.

The Court sided with *Roe* in agreeing that "the unborn have never been recognized in the law as persons in the whole sense." The state "does have an important and legitimate interest in preserving and protecting the health of the pregnant woman," the Court noted, though this interest did not allow the state to "override the rights of the pregnant woman that are at stake." The state's interest and the woman's rights both grew substantially as the pregnancy approached term, the opinion noted, and each becomes "compelling" at a certain point. This presentation framed the Court's attempt to delineate pregnancy along the lines of trimesters, which established that the state's interest started when the first trimester ended.

In conclusion, Justice Blackmun's summary of the majority opinion reiterated that the Texas law as it stood violated a woman's Ninth and Fourteenth Amendment rights.

> Measured against these standards [the Texas law], in restricting legal abortions to those . . . [that save] the life of the mother, sweeps too broadly. The statute makes no distinction between abortions performed early in pregnancy and those performed later, and it limits to a single reason, "saving" the mother's life, the legal justification for the procedure. The statute, therefore, cannot survive the constitutional attack made upon it.

The Court's presentation concluded with Justices White and Rehnquist reading their dissents. It took less than an hour for the Court to deliver the opinion that would reshape every abortion law in the nation—and in the process fuel bitter and sometimes violent controversy—for decades to come.

Chapter 6

The Controversy Continues

MORE THAN A QUARTER of a century after the Supreme Court's watershed ruling, *Roe v. Wade* still embroils the nation in controversy. The decision has been the target of criticism from supporters and opponents alike. Despite its attempt to clarify the rights of women to obtain abortions and the rights of states to regulate them, the opinion did not eliminate the question at the root of the abortion debate: Where does a woman's right to choose end and the fetus's right to life begin?

Fetal Rights

Justice Blackmun, who wrote the Court's majority opinion, and the other justices recognized the difficulty of answering a question so fraught with legal and moral obstacles. Before writing the Court's landmark opinion, Justice Blackmun spent several months doing research at the Mayo Clinic, learning everything he could about pregnancy and abortion. In writing the draft, Justice Blackmun attempted to use the medical knowledge he acquired to craft a balance between the moral and legal issues of abortion. He did this by establishing limits around the state's interest in abortion on the basis of fetal viability. The term, though used often on both sides of the abortion debate, lacked a precise medical definition. In common use, viability simply meant "capable of living."

There were precise divisions for when the state's interest could become compelling, Justice Blackmun wrote: One "is at

Before writing the Court's majority opinion in Roe v. Wade, *Justice Blackmun spent several months researching pregnancy and abortion.*

approximately the end of the first trimester" and the other "is at viability," or the third trimester of pregnancy. At these points, a state may exercise its compelling interest in protecting "potential life" by restricting abortions. The state could not restrict abortion during the first trimester, could intervene only to protect the woman's health during the second trimester, and could intervene to protect the fetus during the third trimester, when the fetus could be capable of life outside the womb.

This delineation seemed clear at the time of the Court's ruling. When Justice Blackmun wrote the majority opinion in *Roe*, babies born before full term often did not survive. With a normal pregnancy culminating in birth at forty weeks, an infant born even four weeks early faced a struggle. Lungs, for example, do not fully develop until the final weeks of gestation.

Medical developments have since made it possible for physicians to save infants born at a gestational age much earlier than anyone dreamed possible in 1973. There have been a few instances of survival for a live birth at twenty-two weeks of gestation. At twenty-four weeks gestational age, an infant has a better than 50 percent chance of survival with intensive hospital care. The odds are nine in ten that infants born during the last two weeks of the second trimester will live.

These medical advances are influencing legislatures and courts as they struggle with the issue of fetal rights. Until the mid-1940s, laws in the United States considered a pregnant woman and her unborn child to be one and the same under the reasoning that the fetus could not survive on its own. Fifty years later, circumstances are different. Significantly preterm infants often require months of care in a neonatal intensive care unit and may face lifelong disabilities. Nonetheless, they are born well before the third trimester of pregnancy that Justice Blackmun identified as the point at which a state might have a compelling interest in protecting the life of the fetus.

Many states now have laws that make injuring or killing a fetus a criminal offense, though in only a few instances have states been successful in prosecuting a fetal death as a murder. The courts have tried to hold women accountable for behavior that inflicts damage on their unborn children, though most such cases are overturned on appeal. Women's rights advocates worry that this trend might lead to government controls aimed specifically at women in areas of life that have long been considered out of bounds for government involvement. Those who support extending full rights to the fetus argue that the fetus has no choice but to be subjected to the mother's actions, and when those actions threaten its existence, the mother's rights must become secondary.

The Roe v. Wade *decision legalized abortion and allowed women to exercise control over their reproductive health.*

Legal Problems with *Roe*

While intended as a compromise between conflicting beliefs about the beginning of life, the Court's potential-life concept blurred the precision the opinion so carefully sought to establish. Despite the solid 7-2 majority the opinion ultimately achieved among the Court's members, Justice Blackmun anticipated that the ruling was more the start of the battle than the end. In a speech at a Chamber of Commerce dinner in Cedar Rapids, Iowa, the day following the Court's release of the ruling, he said,

> The Supreme Court . . . has not authorized abortion on demand. The justices are aware of how sensitive an issue this is and how seemingly insoluble that problem is. No matter how the Court ruled, it will be excoriated from one end of the country to the other.

Since *Roe v. Wade*, most states have passed laws to regulate abortion within the boundaries the opinion established. Fifteen states and the District of Columbia did not repeal their old laws even though *Roe* keeps the states from enforcing them. In some states, this was intentional defiance by legislatures that resented the Court's intrusion into the states' rights to reflect the interests and will of the people. Three states—Alabama, Arizona, and Louisiana—have passed laws that would immediately prohibit abortion if *Roe v. Wade* is ever overturned. Legal experts differ on the validity of these efforts.

Two states, Louisiana and Utah, passed laws intended to challenge *Roe v. Wade* through the courts. These restrictive laws, which have since been found unconstitutional, banned abortions in nearly all circumstances. The states' legislatures have passed declarations of intent to protect an unborn fetus as a person under state law. Because declarations are not laws, however, they do little more than publicly proclaim the states' strong disagreement with *Roe*.

Numerous court cases have sought to redefine and even overturn *Roe v. Wade*. Several succeeded in narrowing the initial decision, though none has as yet resulted in overturning the ruling.

Two that have been particularly influential are *Webster v. Reproductive Health Services* and *Planned Parenthood of Southeastern Pennsylvania v. Casey.*

Webster v. Reproductive Health Services

Many legal and social analysts view the 1989 case *Webster v. Reproductive Health Services* as the Supreme Court's first major departure from *Roe v. Wade.* In reaction to *Roe,* and in deference to what it felt were the wishes of its citizens, the Missouri state legislature passed a law stating that human life begins at conception. The law prohibited the use of state property for performing abortions and required viability tests in advanced pregnancies where the woman desired an abortion.

A close ruling, 5-4, let the Missouri law stand, signaling the Court's first significant departure from *Roe.* Justice Rehnquist wrote the majority opinion that invalidated the trimester viability framework of *Roe.* He had opposed this framework in his *Roe v. Wade* dissension. It put the Court in the position of writing the law, Justice Rehnquist felt, when the Court's role should be only to interpret the law.

In abandoning the trimester structure of *Roe,* Justice Rehnquist drafted the *Webster* opinion to give the state a compelling interest in the life of the fetus throughout pregnancy, not just in its last three months. This would mean that states could impose restrictions on abortion from conception to birth.

Like Justice Rehnquist, Justice Sandra Day O'Connor viewed the trimester framework as flawed. Unlike Justice Rehnquist, however, she did not equate its demise with giving states full control over abortion. Justice O'Connor believed that states have the right to restrict abortions once the fetus can live on its own outside the uterus. Before that point, however, the woman retains the right to an abortion. Justice O'Connor refused to join the majority in granting states unlimited control over abortion. As a result, this point was stricken from the final opinion. *Webster* gave the states greater, but not complete, discretion in determining when they had a "compelling" interest to protect the fetus, and it reaffirmed a woman's right to abort a nonviable fetus.

Justice Sandra Day O'Connor was a key influence in the Webster v. Reproductive Health Services *decision.*

Planned Parenthood of Southeastern Pennsylvania v. Casey

The state of Pennsylvania was among those to react to *Webster.* In 1990, it passed an abortion law implementing stringent requirements including a twenty-four-hour waiting period, informed consent, parental consent for minors, record-keeping procedures, and spousal notification (telling the woman's husband that she was about to undergo an abortion). In another close decision, again 5-4, the Court upheld all but the spousal notification requirement. In what was perhaps its most significant action, the Court this time implemented an "undue burden" standard. Under this standard, wrote Justices O'Connor, Kennedy, and Souter in the Court's opinion, states could not place "substantial obstacles in the path of a woman seeking an abortion before the fetus attains viability."

The Court abandoned the trimester framework that formed the backbone of the *Roe* decision. In its place, the justices extended the concept of potential life introduced in *Roe*. They stated that viability was more a matter of fetal development than the calendar. The state could implement procedures intended to provide complete information about abortion, including alternatives. At the same time, they cautioned, the state had an equal obligation to safeguard a woman's right to choose abortion. Efforts to inform could not impede a woman's attempt to obtain an abortion. The opinion noted,

> *Roe*'s rigid trimester framework is rejected. To promote the State's interest in potential life throughout pregnancy, the State may take measures to ensure that the woman's choice is informed. Measures designed to advance this interest should not be invalidated if their purpose is to persuade the woman to choose childbirth over abortion. These measures must not be an undue burden on the right.
>
> As with any medical procedure, the State may enact regulations to further the health or safety of a woman seeking an abortion, but may not impose unnecessary health regulations that present a substantial obstacle to a woman seeking an abortion.

Pennsylvania governor William Casey speaks to the media after the Planned Parenthood of Southeastern Pennsylvania v. Casey *case.*

The justices concluded the Court's opinion with yet another affirmation that the Court had not changed the intent and meaning of *Roe*. They emphasized that states could not use the potential-life concept to prohibit abortions before the point of viability, writing in the opinion,

> Adoption of the undue burden standard does not disturb *Roe*'s holding that, regardless of whether exceptions are made for particular circumstances, a State may not prohibit any woman from making the ultimate decision to terminate her pregnancy before viability.

In his intense and articulate dissent, Justice Blackmun voiced his concerns that his colleagues were missing the key constitutional aspects of the abortion issue. He argued that any attempt by a state to restrict abortion interfered with a woman's right to choose abortion and consequently with her right to privacy.

> When the State restricts a woman's right to terminate her pregnancy, it deprives a woman of the right to make her own decision about reproduction and family planning— critical life choices that this Court long has deemed central to the right to privacy. The decision to terminate or continue a pregnancy has no less an impact on a woman's life than decisions about contraception or marriage. Because motherhood has a dramatic impact on a woman's educational prospects, employment opportunities, and self-determination, restrictive abortion laws deprive her of basic control over her life. For these reasons, "the decision whether or not to beget or bear a child" lies at "the very heart of this cluster of constitutionally protected choices."

Justice Blackmun also raised the issue of gender equality, a concern of intense interest by the 1990s. When it restricts abortion, Justice Blackmun argued, the state also forces a woman to use her body in ways the state wants her to use it, without compensation. This, he said, triggered the "protection of the Equal Protection Clause." While Justice Blackmun's comments failed to sway his judicial colleagues, they did bring another dimension, equal rights between women and men, to bear on the abortion issue. What effect that will have remains to be seen.

Grassroots Efforts to Change Public Opinion About Abortion

The courtroom was not the only scene for abortion battles. Groups on both sides of the debates organized at the grassroots level, staging protests and rallies. Those who supported a woman's right to choose abortion began referring to their position as pro-choice; those who opposed abortion called themselves pro-life.

Enthusiastic abortion opponents often organized small protests outside clinics and hospitals that provided abortion services. They tried to give pamphlets and other materials to women entering the facilities. Emotions ran high in such settings, and frequently protesters attempted to prevent patients and employees from going into the building. Abortion supporters

Roe v. Wade *continues to ignite controversy among Americans. Here, young people protest abortion at the Supreme Court on the twenty-third anniversary of the decision.*

AMERICAN PUBLIC OPINION ON ABORTION

More Americans support abortion than not, though general public support for abortion varies according to the reason. In a 1992 public opinion poll conducted by *Time*/CNN, about 80 percent of those questioned answered "yes" when asked if they support abortion when the mother's life is at stake or health in danger, and in situations of rape or incest. Support drops to 70 percent if an abortion is sought because the fetus has serious birth defects or is unlikely to survive after birth. Just 47 percent of those questioned said "yes" when asked if they supported abortion for any reason during the first trimester.

Studies show that more than half of all pregnancies in this country are unintended, and more than half of those end in induced abortion. American women obtained 31 million legal abortions between 1973, when *Roe v. Wade* legalized the procedure, and 1997, making abortion the option of choice for dealing with unintended pregnancy. Nearly 90 percent of the abortions performed take place within the first twelve weeks of pregnancy, before the fetus achieves viability. Researchers estimate that at current rates, four in ten American women will have at least one abortion by age forty-five.

retaliated by forming counterprotests that often turned into shouting matches.

In some cases, the emotional pitch of the debate has risen to dangerous levels. Since 1977, antiabortion extremists have set fire to more than one hundred clinics and threatened hundreds more. Police reports document invasions and vandalism at more than five hundred other clinics. One group staged prominent and sometimes violent blockades of abortion clinics in Atlanta during the 1988 Democratic National Convention. The group expanded its tactics to other cities during the following year, resulting in more than twenty thousand arrests for civil disobedience and other charges. The violence has even escalated to murder, with individual activists attacking physicians, clinic workers, and their family members.

The 1994 fatal shooting of Dr. David Gunn outside an abortion clinic in Pensacola, Florida, motivated the U.S. Congress to intervene. It passed the Freedom of Access to Clinic Entrances Act. FACE, as the act is known, makes it a federal crime to block access to abortion clinics or to harass patients or staff. Anti-abortion protesters may still picket, but they must stay the defined distance away from clinic entrances. They also must allow patients to pass through without delaying or detaining them. Violators face stiff prison sentences. The law has succeeded in slowing, though not entirely stopping, antiabortion violence.

Is There Middle Ground?

Whether America can find a comfortable compromise on abortion remains to be seen. The issue's volatility rests not only in judicial interpretations but in emotional and moral arenas. With only three members of the *Roe v. Wade* Court remaining, the future of abortion rights will likely rest in the hands of a new Court in a new century. That Court will confront new technologies that further blur the critical issue of fetal viability that is at the core of the abortion rights argument.

Timeline

1821
Connecticut becomes the first state to make abortion a crime.

1860s
Abortion is illegal throughout the United States.

1873
President Ulysses S. Grant signs into law the *Act for the Suppression of Trade in and Circulation of Obscene Literature and Articles of Immoral Use*, which becomes known as the Comstock Law.

1879
Connecticut passes the Barnum Law, making any form of birth control except abstinence illegal.

1960
The birth control pill becomes available in the United States.

1961
The Supreme Court upholds Connecticut's law making birth control devices illegal in *Poe v. Ullman;* Justice Harlan dissents from the majority opinion.

1965
In *Griswold v. Connecticut,* the Supreme Court establishes the penumbra concept and overturns Connecticut's Barnum Law.

1967
Law student Sarah Weddington obtains an illegal abortion in Mexico; Colorado becomes the first state to pass a law permitting abortion for reasons other than to save the mother's life.

1969
Attorneys Sarah Weddington and Linda Coffee meet Norma McCorvey, the woman who will become Jane Roe, in a Dallas coffee shop.

1970
New York, Alaska, Hawaii, and Washington pass laws allowing first trimester abortions without restriction.

March 3, 1970
Linda Coffee files a lawsuit on Jane Roe's behalf in federal dis-

trict court; the suit names Dallas County district attorney Henry Wade as the defendant.

May 22, 1970
Roe v. Wade goes to trial before the Fifth Circuit Court's panel of three federal judges.

June 17, 1970
The Fifth Circuit Court issues a thirteen-page ruling that finds the Texas law prohibiting abortion unconstitutional, but it fails to include an injunction preventing Texas from continuing to enforce the law.

1971
President Richard Nixon signs the law repealing the Comstock Law; the Supreme Court defines a law's use of the term *health* to include psychological as well as physical well-being in its decision in *United States v. Vuitch.*

May 21, 1971
The Supreme Court agrees to hear arguments in *Roe v. Wade* and another abortion case, *Doe v. Bolton.*

September 1971
Justices Hugo Black and John Harlan resign from the Supreme Court for health reasons, leaving two vacancies just weeks before the Court's scheduled session.

December 1971
Congress approves two new justices, Lewis Powell and William Rehnquist.

December 13, 1971
The Supreme Court hears arguments in *Roe v. Wade* and *Doe v. Bolton.*

1972
The Supreme Court's *Eisenstadt v. Baird* opinion overturns state laws restricting distribution of contraceptives.

September 5, 1972
After much internal strife, the Supreme Court decides to reargue the abortion cases.

October 11, 1972

The Supreme Court hears rearguments in *Roe v. Wade* and *Doe v. Bolton.*

January 22, 1973

The Supreme Court issues its opinion upholding the federal district courts' findings that the Texas and Georgia abortion laws are unconstitutional, overturning nearly every state abortion law in existence.

1977

Congress passes the Hyde Amendment banning states from using federal Medicaid funds to pay for abortions.

1989

In *Webster v. Reproductive Health Services,* the Supreme Court rules in favor of a Missouri law prohibiting the use of state property for performing abortions and requiring viability tests for women who desired abortions; the decision is the first major departure from *Roe v. Wade.*

1992

Justice Sandra Day O'Connor introduces the "substantial obstacles" guideline in the Supreme Court's opinion invalidating most of a restrictive Pennsylvania law in *Planned Parenthood of Southeastern Pennsylvania v. Casey;* the guideline replaces the trimester framework established in *Roe v.Wade.*

1994

Congress passes the Freedom of Access to Clinic Entrances Act (FACE), in response to acts of violence targeting abortion clinics.

1995

Norma McCorvey (Jane Roe) publicly announces that she can no longer support abortion and goes to work for a major pro-life organization.

1997

Congress votes to outlaw partial-birth abortions, bans abortion for women in federal prisons, restricts federal employees from choosing health insurance that pays for abortion, and bars U.S. military hospitals overseas from performing abortions on active duty women or dependents.

Glossary

abortifacient: Drug or device that can cause an abortion; includes some common forms of birth control that work by preventing the fertilized egg from implanting in the uterus, such as the birth control pill and the intrauterine device (IUD).

abortion: The interruption of pregnancy; can be spontaneous (miscarriage) or caused by medication or surgery.

affidavit: Written statement given under oath to stand in place of testifying in court.

amendment: Formal change or addition to the U.S. Constitution; two-thirds of the states must ratify, or vote to approve, an amendment.

amicus brief: "Friend of the court" brief, a document filed with a court that presents additional supportive information; each side can submit amicus briefs.

anonymous: Keep an individual's identity secret by referring to him or her under a pseudonym, or false name.

appeal: Legal disagreement with a court decision.

appellate: Court that evaluates appeals of lower court decisions; appeals typically focus on technical points of law or judicial procedure. For example, the *Roe* attorneys were able to appeal their case to an appellate court, in this case the U.S. Supreme Court, because the district court that issued the original ruling failed to grant an injunction to prevent the law it said was illegal from being enforced. This made the ruling technically incomplete.

brief: Legal documents about a case given to a court; briefs typically explain situations and circumstances as background information for the court.

class action: Broadens a lawsuit to include any and all individuals who now face, have faced in the past, or will face in the future the circumstances the lawsuit challenges.

Constitution of the United States (U.S. Constitution): Document of the basic principles, powers, duties, rights, and responsibilities of the U.S. government and citizens; first written in 1787 and amended throughout the country's history.

contraception: Means of preventing a woman from conceiving a child; birth control.

defendant: Person who must respond to a lawsuit; often this is the district attorney in the jurisdiction where the suit is filed.

embryo: The first eight weeks of development following the union of an ovum and a sperm; called a fetus after eight weeks.

enumerated rights: Rights specifically expressed in the Constitution; the right to keep and bear arms is one example.

fetus: An unborn child from eight weeks after fertilization until birth.

fundamental freedom: Right or freedom guaranteed by the U.S. Constitution that state and local governments cannot restrict.

gestational age: The age of a fetus expressed in the amount of time, usually measured in weeks or months, since fertilization; sometimes called fetal age.

Hyde Amendment: Federal law preventing states from using federal Medicaid money to pay for abortions for poor women.

informed consent: Complete explanation of a medical or surgical procedure, including possible complications.

injunction: In legal terminology, an order instructing that a particular behavior or action cease, such as enforcement of a law that a court has determined is unconstitutional.

moot: As a legal term, no longer practical or relevant.

moot court: Mock or practice court where attorneys can prepare their questions and strategies; often observed by other attorneys who offer suggestions and observations.

opinion: In legal terminology, the findings and decisions of a court; in the Supreme Court, the Court issues its rulings in a *majority opinion* usually authored by the chief justice or the most senior justice who is in the majority; justices may also write their own *concurring opinions* (further explanation of the decision) or *dissenting opinions* (explaining disagreement with the Court's majority opinion).

parental consent for minors: In many state laws implemented following *Roe v. Wade,* a requirement that a physician receive permission from one or both parents before performing an abortion on a minor; the Supreme Court has allowed certain parental consent requirements to stand in some states.

plaintiff: Person who brings a lawsuit.

reargument: In legal terminology, presenting an appeal a second time.

remedy: As a legal term, the ability to take a concern or dispute to court for resolution.

spousal notification: In many state laws implemented following *Roe v. Wade,* a requirement that a physician tell a woman's husband that the woman plans to undergo an abortion; the Supreme Court generally finds these restrictions unconstitutional.

standing: As a legal term, elements that make a lawsuit valid.

statute: Legal term for a law that has been passed by a legislature.

trimester: One of the three stages of pregnancy which is roughly equal in time; generally divided according to the development of the fetus; generally an unborn child is not viable until the third trimester. *Roe v. Wade* used a trimester framework to delineate when states might have a compelling interest in protecting the life of the unborn child by restricting abortion.

"undue burden" standard: Requirements imposed by state law that "place significant obstacles" in the path of a woman who wants an abortion; examples include multiple-physician consultation, long waiting periods, forced counseling about alternatives to abortion, and other efforts to delay or prevent a woman's access to abortion; arose from a Supreme Court opinion in *Planned Parenthood of Southeastern Pennsylvania v. Casey.*

unenumerated rights: Rights that the U.S. Constitution implies though does not specifically identify; the right to privacy is one example.

viable: As applies to the unborn child, physically developed enough to live outside the womb; in general, viability is highly unlikely before twenty weeks gestational age.

For Further Reading

Alison Cross, writer and coproducer, *Roe v. Wade*. Videotape. Paramount, 1989. This dramatization of the trial presents *Roe v. Wade* through the perceptions of the people who made it happen. Broadcast on NBC network television in 1989, this video is closed-captioned for the hearing-impaired.

JoAnn Bren Guernsey, *Abortion: Understanding the Controversy*. Minneapolis: Lerner Publications, 1993. This book presents a well-balanced examination of the various medical and legal aspects of abortion. It also discusses the implications of *Roe v. Wade* and other significant Supreme Court decisions.

Norma McCorvey with Andy Meisler, *I Am Roe—My Life, Roe v. Wade, and Freedom of Choice*. New York: HarperCollins, 1994. In this autobiography, the woman who became Jane Roe tells her story and offers her perspective on the Supreme Court decision that changed a nation.

Leonard A. Stevens, *The Case of Roe v. Wade*. New York: G. P. Putnam's Sons, 1996. This book examines the people, events, and legal questions of *Roe v. Wade* and other Supreme Court decisions about abortion. It includes a look at the disputes and personality clashes among the justices that resulted in the Supreme Court's decision to reargue the case.

Sarah Weddington, *A Question of Choice*. New York: G. P. Putnam's Sons, 1992. Lead *Roe* attorney Sarah Weddington recalls the trial and her role in it in this autobiography.

Works Consulted

Books

Cynthia R. Daniels, *At Women's Expense: State Powers and the Politics of Fetal Rights.* Cambridge, MA: Harvard University Press, 1993. Political science professor Cynthia Daniels examines efforts by state legislatures to use fetal rights as an avenue to restrict abortion

Ronald Dworkin, *Freedom's Law: The Moral Reading of the American Constitution.* Cambridge, MA: Harvard University Press, 1996. This book looks at the moral and ethical aspects of the U.S. Constitution from the context of its writers' intentions as well as contemporary social issues.

Marian Faux, *Roe v. Wade: The Untold Story of the Landmark Supreme Court Decision That Made Abortion Legal.* New York: Macmillan, 1988. Using interviews conducted in the mid-1980s with the people involved in *Roe v. Wade,* this analysis provides a retrospective view of the case and its events.

David J. Garrow, *Liberty and Sexuality: The Right to Privacy and the Making of Roe v. Wade.* New York: Macmillan, 1994. This Pulitzer Prize–winning author has written and edited a number of books about significant social issues. In this book, he presents a comprehensive examination of *Roe v. Wade* and abortion in the larger contexts of personal freedom and social dynamics.

Jethro K. Lieberman, *The Evolving Constitution.* New York: Random House, 1992. This book examines the shifts in judicial interpretation of the U.S. Constitution that have taken place through the more than two hundred years of its existence.

Roe v. Wade, the Complete Text of the Official US Supreme Court Decision. Annotated by Bo Schambelan. Philadelphia: Running Press, 1992. This book presents the Supreme Court's majority, concurring, and dissenting opinions in *Roe v. Wade.*

Bernard Schwartz, *A History of the Supreme Court.* New York: Oxford University Press, 1993. Noted scholar and historian Bernard Schwartz condenses more than two centuries of the

U.S. Supreme Court into a single, comprehensive book, drawn from notes and memoirs written by and about the men and women who have shaped judicial history.

Laurence H. Tribe, *Abortion: A Clash of Absolutes*. New York: W. W. Norton, 1992. With his experience presenting cases to the Supreme Court as a backdrop, Laurence Tribe explores the opposing viewpoints at either end of the abortion debate and looks at ways to achieve a balance between them.

Periodicals

Eric S. Adler, "The Political Observer: Aborting Intelligent Discussion on Choice," *Wharton Journal*, November 6, 1995.

F. Barringer, "U.S. Ratio of Abortions Is Lowest Since Late '70s," *New York Times*, December 19, 1992.

J. Blenshoof, "*Planned Parenthood v. Casey*, the Impact of the New Undue Burden Standard on Reproductive Health Care," *Journal of the American Medical Association*, May 5, 1993.

William Booth, "California Court Reverses Abortion Law," *Washington Post*, August 6, 1997.

"Change of Heart?" *People Daily*, August 12–13, 1995.

"Court Reaffirms *Roe* but Upholds Restrictions," *Family Planning Perspectives*, July/August 1992.

Douglas Frantz, "The Rhetoric of Terror," *Time*, March 27, 1995.

Michelle Green, "The Woman Behind *Roe v. Wade*," *People Weekly*, May 22, 1989.

S. K. Henshaw and K. Kost, "Abortion Patients in 1994–1995: Characteristics and Contraceptive Use," *Family Planning Perspectives*, July/August 1996.

S. K. Henshaw and K. Kost, "Parental Involvement in Minors' Abortion Decisions," *Family Planning Perspectives*, September/October 1992.

G. Kolata, "Under Pressures and Stigma, More Doctors Shun Abortion," *New York Times*, January 8, 1990.

"A New Chink in *Roe v. Wade*," *Time*, June 17, 1996.

"Report: Abortions Now Offered in First Week of Pregnancy," CNN, December 21, 1997.

"Senate Falls Short of Veto-Proof Margin on Abortion Ban," *Congressional Quarterly*, May 20, 1997.

"A Stunning Approval for Abortion," *Time*, February 5, 1973.

A. Torres and J. D. Forrest, "Why Do Women Have Abortions?" *Family Planning Perspectives*, July/August 1988.

David Van Biema, "An Icon in Search Mode," *Time*, August 21, 1995.

David Van Biema, "Keep Your Distance," *Time*, July 11, 1994.

"Woman Behind *Roe vs. Wade* Alters Abortion View," Reuters (syndicated news report), August 12, 1995.

Internet Resources

Abortion Law Homepage (http://members.aol.com/abtrbng/) This website provides background information and links to legal opinions about abortion. The status of abortion laws in various states is frequently updated. Some material, including key Supreme Court opinions, is available for download in rich-text format. The site also contains the syllabus, or summary, that Justice Blackmun read during the Court's public announcement of its *Roe v. Wade* opinion.

Alan Guttmacher Institute (http://www.agi-usa.org) AGI conducts unbiased health research, policy analysis, and public education about sexual activity, contraception, abortion, and child bearing. The website contains extensive statistical information as well as analytical articles about trends and issues in reproductive health.

Centers for Disease Control and Prevention (http://www.cdc.gov/cdc.html) The CDC is an agency of the U.S. Department of Health and Human Services that monitors a wide range of health-related information. The CDC's home page offers links to additional resources, including the National Center for Health Statistics, which collects and reports data such as abortion rates.

First Amendment Center (http://www.fac.org/default.asp) This website covers legal matters from around the United States that are related to the rights guaranteed by the Constitution in the First Amendment. The site is updated frequently, and it contains material about state, federal, and appellate court actions.

Historic Supreme Court Decisions (http://supct.law.cornell. edu/supct/cases/topic.htm) Sponsored by Cornell University School of Law, this website contains texts of the full opinions (majority, concurring, dissenting) of dozens of significant U.S. Supreme Court decisions. Use the "next" and "previous" buttons to page through the listings, which are in chronological order. The site has *Roe v. Wade* as well as other relevant cases that contributed to the Court's findings.

Priests for Life (http://www.priestsforlife.org/index2.html) An association of Catholic clergy sponsors this website, which offers assistance and information about abortion and euthanasia in support of the Catholic Church's pro-life teachings. Among the materials found here are interviews with Norma McCorvey (Jane Roe) and Sandra Cano (Mary Doe in *Doe v. Bolton*).

Pro-Choice Home Page (http://www.prochoice.com/) This website provides information and resources about abortion alternatives. This site also includes an interview with Sandra Cano (Mary Doe in *Doe v. Bolton*).

Reproductive Rights (http://www.aclu.org/issues/reproduct/ arrr.html) The American Civil Liberties Union (ACLU) sponsors this website, which provides information about the legal status of various antiabortion efforts. It also has material describing the ACLU's pro-choice position on reproductive rights, including birth control and abortion.

Index

Picture Credits

About the Author

Deborah S. Romaine specializes in writing about health-related topics. She has a master's degree in English and creative writing from the University of Washington. Ms. Romaine has published more than three hundred articles and has coauthored or ghost-written several books. A former corporate trainer, she also teaches creative and business writing. Ms. Romaine is an avid bicyclist and amateur classical guitarist. She lives with her husband and two children in Tacoma, Washington.